T0065722

I RANT THEREFORE I AM

Books by Dennis Miller

The Rants
Ranting Again

I RANT THEREFORE I AM

Dennis Miller

Broadway Books

New York

BROADWAY

First Broadway Books trade paperback edition published 2001.

Designed by Lisa Sloane

The Library of Congress has cataloged the hardcover as:

Miller, Dennis, 1953–
I rant, therefore I am / Dennis Miller— 1st ed.
p.   cm.
1. American wit and humor.   I. Title: I rant, therefore I am.   II. Title.
PN6162 .M4893 2000
814'.54—dc21   99-055833

ISBN-13: 978-0-767-90575-6

146712470

For Carolyn (Ali), Holden, and Marlon-Olivier.
You are the loves of my life.

Contents

Preface

Rant, Therefore I Am originally appeared on my HBO show "Dennis Miller Live." I'd like to thank Jose Arroyo, David Feldman, Eddie Feldman, Jim Hanna, Leah Krinsky, Jacob Weinstein, and David Weiss for their assistance. I'd also like to thank Amy Scheibe and Chris Min at Doubleday, Michele DeVoe, Colleen Grillo, Marc Gurvitz, Kirsten McFarland, Debbie Palacio, Kevin Slattery, and, I'd especially like to thank all my friends at HBO, with a special thanks to Jeff Bewkes, Chris Albrecht, Carolyn Strauss, and Sarah Condon, who make it all possible. Now, I don't want to get off on a rant here, but . . .

I RANT
THEREFORE
I AM

Talk Shows

Now, I don't want to get off on a rant here, but daytime TV talk shows have become a vast, fetid, sump-sucking wasteland, populated by a parade of circus geeks and sideshow oddities that would have given even Federico Fellini a case of grade-A, toss-in-your-sleep, ate-a-garlic-cheese-and-sushi-calzone-right-before-bedtime nightmares. And that's just the hosts.

With everything that's on daytime television today, one thought continues to haunt me: How in the hell did Richard Bey get canceled?

Lest anyone think I'm biting the hand that feeds me, let me clarify: When I speak of talk shows, I mean the anti-Darwinian, *Lord of the Flies* cluster-fucks that pass for daytime programming. The shows where the basic rules of human discourse are paid about as much attention as Linda Hunt on the set of "Baywatch."

Now, I'm not saying they all suck like airplane toilets, but you could safely conclude that the good ones can be counted on the one hand of a bad wood shop teacher.

It's not hard to figure out why these shows are popular. They answer the burning question: "What do the people we see being arrested on 'Cops' do during the day?"

Why have these daytime chatfests flourished? Well, the answer is that all the smart people are working when this shit is on. The submorons who watch this dreck are the people nobody wants to hire.

That's the only way I can explain the sheer number of gene pool skimmings that make it on the air. I swear, you can still see the jelly on their foreheads where the electroshock terminals were attached. And what I find so scary is that some of these shows have been on for years but they still manage to find this *Fantasia* broom army of social misfits to appear on them. They all look like they've just stepped out of a William Faulkner rough draft, mouth-breathing freaks who make Jethro Bodine look like David Niven.

But these shows *do* provide a service. They weave together some of the shabbier threads in the fabric of our society and give them a voice . . . even if that voice is frequently only heard in their own heads. Hey, how many times have I seen chunky tattooed women slap-fighting in the Laundromat parking lot and wished I knew the back story?

And the Yoda of Daytime, the Professor Emeritus of emotional chum, is one Jerry Springer, Esquire. Now, here's a man who has become a household name . . . make that a trailer-hold name, by offering daily spectacles that make Brazilian snuff films seem uplifting by comparison.

Each day Springer ladles through the primordial ooze like some psychotic cafeteria lady and dishes up the mystery meat of the human condition.

My favorite part of the Jerry Springer show is Jerry's "Final Thought." Yeah, like all of a sudden Jerry is going to add some perspective and sanity to tie it all together. I got news for you. Jerry has only one final thought. And you know what that is? "Are the Siamese-Twin Hasidic Skinheads confirmed for tomorrow?"

We are the rubberneckers and Springer and his ilk orchestrate the train wrecks we all slow down to ogle. And the freak stakes have to be jacked up higher with each passing day because, let's face it, folks, we are less shockable than David Lynch in a pair of platform galoshes.

Well, that just about wraps this rant up, but here's my final thought. What kind of world would it be if we weren't all inexorably drawn to watching trashy chicks scream at each other right before they get a makeover that looks like it was done by a guy who paints murals on the sides of vans, only to find out that no amount of makeover will be enough to assuage their pain at losing their man to another ho's hoochie?

Of course, that's just my opinion, I could be wrong.

The Social Responsibility of the President

As originally aired on 1/30/98

Now, I don't want to get off on a rant here, but our current Commander in Chief seems to have yet again raised the bar for questionable behavior. As a matter of fact, Hillary Clinton hears the words "I'm sorry" more frequently than Pauly Shore on "Celebrity Jeopardy."

You know, I feel a bit of sympathy for Hillary. But she's obviously known about this kind of stuff for years and made some peace with it. And I even feel a little sorry for Clinton himself because truth be told, none of our lives would stand up to this high-powered X-ray scrutiny. But the fact is, he chose the fishbowl, undoubtedly so he could grope the plastic mermaid seated on the little treasure chest.

Clinton's recent scandal is reminiscent of Nixon's Watergate, if for no other reason than each President's main mistake was the firing of Cox. You see, until the other "tricky dick" was asked to leave the table, no President had ever quit and we weren't sure our system could survive it. Well, now we know it can.

But it's not as if getting caught really matters, does it? Clinton's most recent approval rating is 73 percent. Can you grasp that figure, 73 percent?

You cannot get 73 out of 100 people to agree on whether or not they like themselves. Now these figures, of course, could spiral downward if more women step forward or obstruction of justice is proven or, even more importantly, if the stock market suddenly does a Lewinsky.

But the President's amazing approval rating would seem to indicate that we are now prepared to accept the sexual foibles of those who seek public office. Why not go all the way? Instead of names on the ballots, why don't we just make our decisions based on Polaroids of all the candidates' genitalia? It wouldn't be that different, really. Some are to the left, some to the right. Some represent bigger government and some, unfortunately, smaller government.

You know, maybe the reason we're more forgiving nowadays is because it's finally sunk in these are just guys.

Guys who at some point are presumptuous enough to lift their head off the pillow in outback towns like Little Rock, Arkansas, lean over, and tell their wife that they've decided it's their turn to become the most powerful man in the world. And the only difference between you and them is that their wife doesn't say, "Ah shut up, you asshole. How's about gettin' the day shift at Meineke first, okay?"

But even if we all are in a more forgiving mood, I think we have to draw the line at this guy and his handlers steamrolling this young girl now just because she let *Air Force One* buzz her tower. Okay? For Christ's sake, she was twenty-one years old. In all honesty, a twenty-one-year-old should want to blow the President, okay? This kid's life should not be ruined now, just because the President views the White House intern population in the same way he views the chicken-fried steak steam table at a Luby's Cafeteria. But unfortunately, Clinton and his wingtipped thugs have to win, and that means Monica Lewinsky will join the others who have been immolated on the pyre of Bill Clinton's ambition.

Stoking the flames will be presidential arsonist James Carville, a snake oil salesman who actually looks like a snake. Is it just me or is this guy harder to watch than sausage being made? Huh? Carville's got more nervous tics than a Belfast parking valet.

Hey, let's bottom-line this. As far as Clinton's concerned, it all comes back to getting a little tail. Bill Clinton wanted to become President for the same exact reason guys used to drive Day-Glo orange IROC Z-28s in the seventies.

And Bill Clinton will be able to get out of this. You mark my words. He always does. This guy has hung off more cliffs than an Austrian with an inner ear infection. He is the modern-day Prometheus, picked apart by the media vultures each day only to become whole again to weather yet another scandal.

Maybe we root for him because he is our Rocky, taking punch after punch after punch, round after round, and always calling out for his Adrian. The only difference is, you know this as well as I do, Clinton is also trying to nail all the ring girls.

Of course, that's just my opinion, I could be wrong.

Work-Obsessed People

ow, I don't want to get off on a rant here, but we seem to be working a little too hard lately here in the Good Old U.S. of Type A.

To many work-obsessed Glengarrys these days, nine to five is considered part-time.

People can't even relax on vacation anymore. They flop around like Ned Beatty's man-tits on a trampoline. That image might send me back to therapy. You know, most workaholics have the attention span of Farrah Fawcett at a Wagner opera, or, for that matter, the Letterman show.

A lot of this is due to the fact that the two-career couple is no longer a luxury, but a necessity. An average American family just can't survive on one salary anymore. Not if you want to have the essentials—basic cable, premium cable, a DirectTV satellite dish, and, oh yeah, food. Like Rice-A-

Roni, the San Francisco Treat . . . San Francisco . . . cable cars . . . cable! May the circle be unbroken . . .

But somewhere along the line Americans decided that work could actually be fun. I believe psychologists describe this as the condition in which the person being held hostage actually falls in love with the person who's kidnapped them.

For Americans, work is what the pub is to the British, the vodka cellar is to the Russians, and what any place but the shower is to the French.

Every company has at least one Type A jag-off, the freak with the coffee mug that says TGIM on it. Power-suited desk jockeys charging ahead at a pace that makes Teddy Roosevelt look like a Rasta in an ether factory. They are simply grown-up versions of the kids who would raise their hands at the end of the last class before Christmas break and remind the teacher that she forgot to assign homework.

What gets me is that you never see workaholics where they can do you some good. I mean, where are all the go-getters at the DMV, huh? Why does a visit to the post office always seem like an underwater Tai Chi class?

Hell, I'll be honest, I dream of a day when we are all replaced by computers. I can't wait until my entire presence on my show can be achieved simply by plugging in the Smugatron 2000 and pointing a camera at it.

But I guess, truth be told, in some sense, we are all workaholics, because getting through life is a hard job.

Keeping a marriage together, raising children, and maintaining friendships—it's all hard work.

That's why whenever I spend any appreciable time now with my family, well, I insist that they, uh, they cut me a check. I find I try harder when they pay me. I don't take my loved ones for granted anymore because the money that they give to me shows me that they don't take me for granted. And the more money I get from them, the more of me they are going to get from me.

But who is a workaholic? Here are some hints.

1. When you're making a phone call from home, you hit "9" to get out.

2. You know you're a workaholic when you refer to your wife's vagina as "the in-box."

3. You're so pale from sitting in the office that people keep telling you they loved you in *Powder*.

4. You're so busy you have to pencil in a shit.

And finally, you know you're a workaholic if, in spite of the fact that you've been transferred to a five-sided building across the river, you still stop by on weekends to give your old boss an Arkansas howdy.

Of course, that's just my opinion, I could be wrong.

The End of Privacy

Now, I don't want to get off on a rant here, but if you get the funny feeling you're being watched, well, that's going into your file.

Hey, when did our national anthem change from "The Star-Spangled Banner" to "Every Breath You Take"? In this grand democracy of ours, where the Statue of Liberty now bears a striking resemblance to Gladys Kravitz from "Bewitched," you've got a better shot at hearing Charlie Sheen deliver the keynote address at a Promise Keepers rally than you do at maintaining anything that even vaguely resembles a private life. Our constitutional rights are currently under more strain than Linda Tripp's capri pants.

Ever since Adam invented the fig-leaf genital toupee, privacy has been a basic human need. And as our lives get more complicated and therefore require even more privacy, the keyhole through which anyone can peer is growing wider than Steven Tyler's dental dam.

Computers now sell our names and addresses to the highest bidder. I get so many catalogs at my house, I had to order a special Hammacher Schlemmer solar-powered catalog lazy Susan to put them all on. You know what Victoria's Secret is, folks? There are no trees left.

Companies are able to find out your spending habits and preferences and junk-mail you accordingly. I mean, how else would Lillian Vernon know that I happen to have a fetish for musical toilet paper rolls that play the theme from "M*A*S*H"?

When you fill out a warranty card on a toaster, you seal your consumer fate. You end up on a master toaster list. Everybody that has anything remotely to do with toast is given your name. You get calls from jelly makers, and butter churners, and tea importers, and people who knit I LIKE TOAST toaster covers. You'll eventually get caught up in a toast pyramid scheme, you lose your entire fortune, your house, your family, and you know what? You're toast.

This El Niño–like erosion of man's natural right to be secure in his own home, to speak with anonymity, and to masturbate like a red-assed monkey watching the banana channel . . . Well, this erosion is sadder than Richard Simmons attempting to throw a football. This is not the America our Founding Fathers envisioned. And I know that for a fact because I read their diaries.

But nowadays, we have the skeleton key to everybody's diary. My God, can you believe that we're actually all aware of the fact that our President's dick is bent? When in the history of mankind have the multitudes known the exact arc and curvature of their leader's staff?

The press has been all over Bill Clinton like fire ants on a half-eaten Yodel. Clinton's trials and tribulations indicate that we have reached the anti-Orwellian juncture where the government isn't violating the privacy of its citizens but rather the citizens are violating the privacy of the government. Hey, if I get any more mock deep, I'm gonna end up reading Spencers Gifts cards on the midway at Lilith Fair.

Hey, truth be told, paranoia is no longer a psychological condition but rather a *keen* perception of one's surroundings. If you have ever expressed an opinion, or possibly fit the profile of a subversive troublemaker, then you can be reasonably assured that your phone is probably more tapped than Toni Braxton's checking account. Hell, my phone line has more clicks than a Ubangi marital spat.

And as the last guy to sneak into the celebrity chamber just before the watertight door slammed shut, I realize I have to adjust my expectations of privacy to the situation. If you see me in some public setting, fine. Approach me, I won't bite. But when you see me at a *Star Trek* convention talking about "The Squire of Gothos" episode with Leonard Nimoy, back off. I'm not there for you, I'm there for me.

But we are not just talking about celebrities anymore. It is the average person whose privacy is being invaded by technology. You feel like a number? Well, take a number.

Of course, that's just my opinion, I could be wrong.

Style vs. Substance

Now, I don't want to get off on a rant here, but style is whupping up on substance like a drill sergeant on a tubby recruit with a sexually ambiguous first name.

As a culture we're becoming so superficial it wouldn't surprise me if the E! Channel now qualified to receive federal funding. We're so fixated on the sprig of parsley and frilly toothpick garnishing the daily special of our mass consciousness, it's completely escaped our notice that all those trimmings are doing is dressing up a plate that's emptier than a NOW benefit where the guest speaker is Tommy Lee.

Style can probably best be described as substance abuse. Because usually substance suffers when style takes the wheel. Except, of course, in the case of Joan and Melissa Rivers. Nobody, and I mean nobody, brings more depth and import to the subject of celebrity clothes, hair, and makeup.

Kudos to you, Joan and Missy, you have tackled a subject that could be misconstrued as frivolous and you make those five hours before the Annual Blockbuster Awards as meaningful as the show itself.

Substance is a support beam, and style is the mirror ball hanging from it. In many cases, style is simply substance displaced. A Humvee squeezing through the jungle of Borneo is a tool. A Humvee squeezing into a parking space on Rodeo Drive is being driven by a tool.

You know, folks, all the money in the world can't buy you substance. Donald Trump has been trying to buy it for years. Sorry, Donny, but when you go that far out of your way to advertise the fact that you're a billionaire, well, you're obviously bankrupt in all the ways that really matter. And by the way, trim those goddamn eyebrows. They're like a sod farm for Paula Cole's armpits.

You know, because we're so entranced by outside appearances, we easily fall for imitations. For example, there's this guy right now who's becoming pretty successful doing what is essentially a pale imitation of me. He's stolen all my moves, he sounds like me, he even looks remarkably like I do, and people are going wild about him. Damn you, Leonardo DiCaprio! Damn you to Hell!

In no other arena does style triumph over substance more than in politics. Now, there was a time when politicians spoke in sound bites. Now they think in them.

In politics, the most blatant deceptions can be perpetrated and then explained away with smooth rhetoric and careful misdirection that leave the American citizens feeling as if nothing happened in the first place. Politicians know that it's better to be good at looking good than it is to actually be good.

Hey, you don't have to look any further than the Oval Orifice to find a man who is more interested in looking good than doing right. That's why President Clinton polls the American people before every major decision, that's why he's more changeable than a colicky baby. Christ, the only time he'd buck the polls is if a majority of the American people told him to do so.

And all this superficiality at the top trickles down and infects the herd. We're so wrapped up in image and style these days, even walking the walk requires special $450 "Walk-the-walk" shoes.

Every decade thinks its clothing styles have substance. But, here's a good rule of thumb. One era's ultimate fashion statement will someday be another era's kitschy Halloween costume.

And it appears much of today's music is also right off the rack. Is it just me or are the Spice Girls one of the biblical signs of Armageddon? Four Carnaby Street pop tarts with a beefed-up karaoke machine who make Milli Vanilli look like Pink Floyd. Can't wait for their *Unplugged* special, huh?

In the style over substance war, Los Angeles is ground zero. You know, there are people in L.A. who've had so many face-lifts they can't attend auctions anymore because every time they smile their arm goes up.

Hey, there are those who would argue that this country was built on dreams, and so illusion is its legacy. Okay, but can't we just split the difference between style and substance? We have to stop living life as if it were a cross between a photo-op and a free-for-all scramble for cheap Mardi Gras beads. Let's launch an all-out campaign to eliminate pretension wherever and whenever we see it. Let's take stun guns to people who use more than six words to order their coffee, okay? . . . Let's suffocate the motherfucker who insists the wine needs to breathe . . . Let's slap down pompous comedians who trick an audience into laughing by gratuitous use of the word "motherfucker" . . . And finally, let's—let's hog-tie Martha Stewart and force-feed her Fatburgers.

Of course, that's just my opinion, I could be wrong.

Money & Greed

You know, folks, Don King is the poster child for greed in this culture, but if you look closely, you can see all of our names listed in the fine print.

Now, I don't want to get off on a rant here, but ever since Midas first discovered that a golden touch precludes masturbation, greed has driven more people than a Bombay bus driver during the opening weekend of Six Flags Over Ganges.

Anyway, with the physical dangers inherent in other forms of excess, greed is the last safe vice. And as we get farther away from the permissiveness of the sixties and seventies, we've become way more interested in mutual funds than we are in mutual orgasms.

Look, I'm just as guilty as the next guy. While looking at the video monitor during my last colonoscopy, I asked the doctor if he could run the Dow Jones ticker across the bottom of the screen.

Money in one form or another has always been around, and so have the less-than-noble feelings that money seems to engender. I'm sure the guy doing abstract expressionist smears of pterodactyl dung on his cave wall was pissed off because the guy in the other cave doing schlocky drawings of mastodons playing poker was driving a Jaguar . . . An actual jaguar.

Look, I've gotta tell ya, I like money. It's neat and tidy and clean. It's fun to fold and stack and smell and look at. It comes in denominations that are easy to keep track of—fives, tens, twenties, hundreds. It's just plain fun to count money and I often do it in a loud falsetto while wearing nothing but a captain's hat and a coin changer.

All right, maybe that's just me, but the point is, it's not what the money represents or what it can buy, it's the money itself I like. The harmony of a five, the balance of a ten, the cute toughness of a nickel, those plucky pennies . . . I just like money. As a matter of fact, I've got a roll of dimes up my ass as you read this. Not a whole roll . . . Just about, yeah, a dollar ten.

Look, let's face facts. Greed is a by-product of a capitalist system. This is the land of possibilities, and we are all free to partake of the many possibilities that are open to us. You can want to live well and still hang on to some principles. Why, take me, for instance. HBO pays me a handsome salary and gives me an absolutely open forum to discuss whatever

I want, week after week. They have no agenda to advance. Sure, HBO could make me its puppet to disseminate whatever ideas they want, along with the high-quality programming and first-rate entertainment that you've come to expect from HBO. But they won't do that. HBO has too much integrity and too much class to do that. So remember, it's not TV. It's HBO.

Given that money is a national obsession, I think we need to take our head out of our assets once in a while and share the wealth. Now, people show their philanthropy in different ways. Ted Turner once gave $1 billion to the United Nations. And last week I donated an Entertainment 2000 coupon book to my kid's school. But not the half-price carnuba wax ticket. Oh, no, that's for Daddy.

And folks, why not give your money away? Not only does it make you feel good, but trying to accumulate the most cash is futile because the game's over, people. Bill Gates has won. Don't even try and beat him. You can't do it. Bill Gates is a white Persian cat and a monocle away from being a villain in a James Bond movie. I mean, the man is worth $90 billion! Apparently a good haircut costs $91 billion.

Hey, look, the general consensus is that what moves man the most is the quest for money. But I happen to believe that man is also moved by a deep sense of honor, and an even deeper sense of doing good.

And once you've achieved that selfless dedication to your fellow man, that cognizance of the fact that we are all interdependent members of the same grand family, well then, then you can hit the lecture circuit and start raking in the cash like a clean whore in Saigon.

Anyway, here are some signs that you might be a little too obsessed with money:

1. You refer to intercourse as "the Horizontal Audit."

2. When in the midst of a dire emergency, you call 911 collect.

3. During a private audience with the Pope, all you can think is "I wonder what this cat's pullin' down?"

And finally, your net worth has more zeros in it than a *Star Trek* convention.

Of course, that's just my opinion, I could be wrong.

The Oscars

As originally aired on 3/20/98

Well, it's T-minus-sixty-or-so hours and counting and then all of our Academy Award questions will be answered. Oh, sure, some things are a given. Billy Crystal will joke about the iceberg in *Titanic* changing its name to something less Jewish. Nicholson might show up shitfaced. And if Gloria Stuart wins for her role as the *Titanic* survivor, she'll no doubt get down on the ground and do ten one-armed push-ups.

Now, I don't want to get off on a rant here, but the Oscars are a cruel reminder that, like the lifeboats on the *Titanic,* if there were enough for everybody there'd be no story. Sure, billions of people watch each year to see the stars and the gowns and to hear the scripted presenter banter that's got all the sparkle and wit of an eye chart, but come on, the real reason the average viewer tunes in is to see rich, beautiful, famous people react to *not* winning in unflinching close-up. That, my friends, is when you really see some Oscar-caliber acting.

And Monday night is just the culmination of Oscar season. For one full month before the actual date, you can't turn on the TV without hearing the word "Oscar" more frequently than Felix Unger's psychotherapist.

Now, I love the Oscars. The glamour, the suspense, the corny speeches—it's a celebration of everything that made me go into showbiz, and I love everything about it. Love, love it, love it, love it, love it. If the Oscars were a hamburger, I'd eat it for breakfast, lunch, and dinner. If the Oscars were a woman, they would now be Mrs. Oscar Miller. In fact, before I have sex with my wife, I paint my entire body gold, and I make her give an acceptance speech, and then if she doesn't climax within thirty seconds, the orchestra starts playing her off.

The fact is that only 5,371 individuals vote on Oscar, and in order to do so you have to be a member of the Academy. What exactly is this Academy we hear so much about? Well, it is a safe and trusting lyceum where acolytes wear white togas and laurel wreaths and are schooled in the subtle nuances of filmmaking and art for art's sake, because, really, in the end, isn't that what Hollywood is all about? Know-what-I-mean, Vern?

And everybody knows that the voting procedure to determine who wins makes the electoral process in Cuba look evenhanded. The criteria for judging what is best are about as objective and rational as Jack Paar on ecstasy. But certain roles are a mortal lock. You want to win an Oscar? Get yourself a part as an alcoholic handicapped hooker on a big ship.

But every year there are incredible films that just some-how get overlooked by the Oscars. This year it was an amazing independent film called *Eve's Bayou*, about a middle-class black family in Louisiana. Hands down, it's one of the best films of the year. But not a single nomination. In past years, it's been movies like *Murder at 1600, Bordello of Blood, Disclosure, The Net,* they were denied. And you know what? There's a common reason why all these films got shafted. Racism.

Seriously, is it just me or are all the nominees this year whiter than an albino mime? I mean, is it not incredible that the sole actor nominated from Steven Spielberg's epic about black slavery *Amistad* is Caucasian? I mean, the only thing that bugs me more than Spike Lee is Spike Lee when he's right.

Anyway, let's review this year's combatants.

L.A. Confidential. Great screenplay, but hey, how can you go wrong when you're working off James Ellroy's classic noir novel. Let's face it, when it comes to authors I've been meaning to read, Ellroy tops them all.

The Full Monty. Hey, if I want to see five fat British asses, I can rent *The Spice Girls Movie*, okay? I'm shithead spice. Now I don't want to give the last scene of *The Full Monty* away, but it would have been nice to see some dick at the very end. I thought it was hypocritical that the actors were willing to show it, but the director felt we didn't deserve it. You see, that's why I liked *Boogie Nights*. We got to see the dick. It's not like I'm dick crazy or anything, trust me, I've seen my share of dicks in locker rooms, in *The Crying Game,* when I interviewed for a White House internship, so my dick passport has been stamped, but I reiterate, if the dick is integral to the movie, as I believe it was in *The Full Monty,* then we should be treated to an extreme close-up of some bangers and mash. Or don't make the movie at all. So yeah, *The Full Monty,* loved it. I just needed to see the dick.

Good Will Hunting. Where do these two little fresh-faced motherfuckers get off being this brilliant this early? Huh? I wonder what their dicks look like.

Titanic. Deserved every nomination it got, except for maybe the special effects thing. And what in the hell is the Academy thinking not nominating Leonardo DiCaprio? In the eighteen times I've been to see this movie, he has got nothing but better. He is a genius. He is a God. Leo, paint me like one of your French girls. I love you, Leo.

As Good As It Gets. Too much gay stuff.

Well, who knows what the 70th Academy Awards will hold. But I'll guarantee you this. If you're looking for justice at the Oscars, you're probably not going to find it.

Because if this were a just world, before the show even started Monday night, the tungsten-steel C-clamp holding the loose skin on the back of Joan Rivers's skull would suddenly blow out and she'd instantaneously unravel into a yapping shar-pei scooting her Vera Wang hind end across the red carpet to hump on Jack Valenti's leg.

Of course, that's just my opinion, I'd like to thank the Academy.

Going Bald

Now, I don't want to get off on a rant here, but in our culture, there is no greater cause of agony, insecurity, or Porsche 911 sales than baldness.

What genetic squirting flower is it that determines which of us ends up looking like Robert Plant and which of us ends up looking like Mel Cooley?

Come on, guys, you know how it works. One day you are standing in front of a mirror with a full head of hair and the next you're trying to get the "most coverage" out of the few hairs you have left, like the guy spreading crushed gravel on your driveway.

There are certain telltale signs that you might be losing your hair that you should be aware of.

If you find yourself actually wondering what baseball cap is appropriate for a funeral.

If you notice your barber just making the clicking noise with the scissors without actually touching your hair.

And if your nickname at work is "Dickhead" and you're a nice guy.

Entire careers have been built on having hair. I'll say it right now. Had I been bald, I never would have gotten this far in show business. I would have had to write for somebody with hair. In fact, that's really what separates the performers from the writers in Hollywood—hair. My entire writing staff is completely hairless. They hate me. But I don't care because they're a bunch of pathetic, bald losers.

But I realize my head gravy days are numbered. The once-bustling downtown of my abundantly populated scalp is becoming a wasteland of burned-out storefronts and boarded-up windows as the occupants move to the outlying suburbs of my neck, ears, and back.

You can try to compensate for your loss in other areas, but the truth is no amount of money or fame will change the fact that you look like the guy who takes the youth group to sing at the nursing home.

When you think about it, hair is all we men have got. We don't have the option of using makeup to hide the flaws in our appearance or enhance our good traits. Once the hair goes, that's it. And then we're faced with the distasteful task of having to cultivate other attributes to make ourselves attractive. And frankly, who's got the time? I mean, I've got a wife, two kids, and golf. My dance card's full enough without my having to go out and get a fucking personality. Okay?

Women will tell you that bald guys are sexy. But they also claim that size doesn't matter. Well, I can assure you that there are very few supermodels out there looking for a bald guy with a tiny dick. Unless, of course, he has coke.

But some women actually *don't* mind baldness. Some women dig it. See, when a woman is in a relationship with a bald guy, she derives security from his insecurity. She knows he's so grateful to her for putting up with what he perceives as his gross defect that he'll never cheat on her. To a woman, her lover's bald spot is like a cattle brand, all right? It's his special mark guaranteeing that if he ever accidentally wanders off the trail, he'll be returned to her for immediate castration.

Now, there are many different ways to soften the blow of nature's defoliating wrath.

The comb-over. This method uses the hair growth that you have on the good side of your head to cover the bad side. You let those few strands of hair grow about six feet long and before you can say "Giuliani," you're spending an hour and a half in the bathroom every morning with two mirrors and a sextant, constructing a Dairy Queen swirl ice cream cone on your head. This works fine until the first breeze hits your baldy bean and your hair unwinds and gets snagged in the spokes of a passing Harley.

Hair paint. Hey, the day I paint my head is the day I need to.

Rogaine. Even if it works for you, if you want to keep your hair, you can never stop using it. Rogaine is the middle-aged equivalent of crack.

Hair plugs. This is where they use donor sites from one spot on your body and transplant them to your head, which is a gradual process that eventually makes you look like a postnuclear Chia pet.

Plugs can cost up to $20,000 and they look about as natural as a cornfield on a hockey rink.

And lastly, the toupee. Wearing a toupee is like covering up a carpet stain with a Day-Glo bean bag chair. My favorite faux hair faux pas is the guy with natural red hair who buys the jet black toupee. It makes his head look like the high water mark on the side of a cargo ship. Guys, trust me. There is no toupee in the world that cannot be spotted by a near-sighted mole with his back turned.

Now, there are all these euphemisms for toupees. Natural hair integration, hair replacement system, follicular restoration placement. Cut to the chase. Why don't we just call them Everybody Knows There's a Fur Divot on Your Head.

And the crème de la crème rinse of toupees is Sammy Donaldson. Sam Donaldson. What is it that possesses Sam to sport a rug that wouldn't be more obvious if Ali Baba was flying on it?

You know, you're damn right there's a cover-up in Washington, Sam. And it's sitting right on your Vulcan spin-art skull. Okay? Quite frankly, I can't even pay attention to what you're saying anymore because I keep waiting for that thing on the top of your head to get up on its hind legs and beg for a peanut.

Of course, that's just my opinion, I could be wrong.

Fear of Flying

hy are so many people afraid to fly when it's such an enjoyable experience? I mean, the wonderful cuisine, the comfortable seats, the friendly and caring flight attendants, the first-rate entertainment, the fresh, healthful cabin air . . . why, I wish I were flying right now!

Truth be told, I'm petrified of air travel. My wife won't even sit next to me on a flight because when I get scared I scratch at the airplane windows like a ferret in an aquarium. There is nothing more embarrassing than breaking down in tears in front of your entire family only to realize the sound you heard was the captain putting down the landing gear.

Now, I don't want to get off on a rant here, but I've been on more bad flights than a one-eyed kamikaze pilot.

My fear of flying starts as soon as I buckle myself in and the guy up front mumbles a few unintelligible words. Then before I know it, I'm thrust into the back of my seat by acceleration that seems way too fast, then we veer immediately into a turn that seems way too sharp, and the rest of the trip is an endless nightmare of turbulence and near-misses . . . then the cabbie drops me off at the airport.

Now, I must navigate the labyrinthine baffle chamber of security checkpoints manned by elite professionals who were drummed out of the mall cop academy because they were caught filching tiny Gouda wheels and bits of Cotto salami from the 3-D Hickory Farms simulator that all students must train on.

Hey, who better to do a cavity search than an asshole? By the way, if you feel you're at risk for a cavity search, my advice is to have some fun with it, put some stuff up there for them to find. Your high school ring, a roll of Mentos, or a note that says: YOU'RE GETTING WARMER.

It kinda humanizes the whole process.

Then it's time to board the plane. Once you've nestled into your seat, which was last cleaned by the Earth-bound third Wright Brother, Noodles, and you've arranged your minuscule stinky synthetic car wash shammy of a blanket and your Stay Free pillow pad that's the size and softness of a geltab multivitamin, and adjusted to the jet cold, tuberculosis-microbe-laden recirculated air that's blowing right down your spine, you've now achieved the comfort level of a North Korean POW with an ingrown toenail and no premium cable.

And keep in mind all of this discomfort occurs before the real fun starts. Before the 125-ton metal tube goes up into the sky. Now, maybe you're one of those stat monkeys who insist that flying is safer than driving. Yeah, maybe, but how often do you see airplane collisions where afterward the pilots are able to exchange insurance information?

Is there any other activity besides air travel that combines so many different elements of unpleasantness in so many varying degrees? What else affords you the opportunity to sample from an emotional smorgasbord containing everything from mere boredom to abject terror, along with a dazzling assortment of physical maladies ranging from dehydration to projectile flatulence and a neck that is stiffer than a seventeen-year-old Amish kid at a strip club?

Every flight I'm on there's a screaming baby. Me. And the thing that makes me most nervous about flying is the other passengers. When I watch a fucking moron try for ten minutes to stuff a Jet Ski into an overhead bin, I am overwhelmed by the fallibility of all humankind and I realize that the engineers who designed the plane, the pilots, and the air traffic controllers all share in the same fakokta genetic code.

Now, I don't want to just whine about flying without offering some constructive solutions. Here's a tip on how to deal with your fear of flying. I've told my wife and my manager not to tell me if I'm supposed to fly somewhere. Then a team of men comes to my house in the middle of the night, kidnaps me, puts me in a large pet carrier, and keeps me sedated until I get to my destination.

Another suggestion is to try talking to the person next to you . . . Unless it's me . . . Then shut the fuck up. Because I am filled with anxiety and I will chill you like a head of lettuce because I'm too nervous to be interested in what you do for a living, okay? It's nothing personal, I'm sure you're very nice, I just don't want the last words I utter in this life to be, "Wow, aluminum siding, that's great . . ."

Also you should know that if you are seated in the exit row, you had better be ready to move and move fast because if you miss a step you are going to have a Dennis Miller–sized hole right through your ass. All right? I'm not willing to have my vital organs cooked al dente just because I drew the short straw on the seating chart.

Hey, bottom line, the problem with flying is that it is not a natural state of affairs. The first time we get on a plane we all have that look on our face like a donkey being airlifted in a sling out of a flooded ravine.

Now you add to that the fact that there's something very cocky and presumptuous about three hundred humans taunting God and nature by eating bad lasagna and drinking screw-top wine while adjusting their headphones to better hear the audio track of *Dunston Checks In,* all the while barreling along at 600 mph at 32,000 feet.

Hey, come to think of it, no wonder God invented clear air turbulence. If you were the supreme being of the universe, wouldn't you keep everybody in line by occasionally jostling the shit out of all these uppity punks like we were Michael Flatley's nut sack?

Of course, that's just my opinion, I could be wrong.

Capital Punishment

Has anybody else noticed how the death penalty is becoming a way of life in this country? Texas is executing so many prisoners now they've erected a ticking sign like the one outside the Hard Rock Cafe.

Now, I don't want to get off on a rant here, but the reason it's called capital punishment is that it's a capital idea. It's reserved for those we deem the worst of the worst, the curdled cream of the crop, humans possessed of an evil so malignant, so virulent, and indeed so original that their continued existence is an insult to the rest of us.

Critics of the death penalty say that when we execute a murderer then we as a society are no better than he is. Hey, I'm not an elitist snob, I don't think I'm better than anyone. So fry the motherfucker.

On the other hand, executing a human being, no matter how hopelessly broken he or she is, is not a fun or an easy thing, but I believe that sometimes it has to be done for the good of society. Could I personally throw the switch? Well, say in the case of Tim McVeigh, yeah. I believe I could do him with a bucket of water and a bad extension cord. And really I don't say that with any degree of joy but rather with the resolute knowledge that this is how it has to be. We can't live with you, Tim, you can't live with us, sorry it didn't work out, see you at God's place.

It's not that I'm not open-minded about the issue. I liked the movie *Dead Man Walking* and it made me think. Because Susan Sarandon was really hot and she was also a nun. So does that mean I'm, like, attracted to a nun?

If there is a problem with capital punishment in this nation, it's that we try to be too civilized about it. It doesn't surprise me that statistics often show that the death penalty is not a deterrent to crime. I believe our half-stepping when it comes to meting out the ultimate spanking softens the psychological blow necessary to drive the consequence nail home.

It's no mystery why we try to find the least painful way to whack our psychos. We think it's humane. We automatically assume that we are elevated in stature by replacing the mayhem of violent death with a clean, quiet, clinical hum. We allow the condemned "60 Minutes" interviews, favorite meals, and an appeals process that drags out longer than Porky Pig singing "Hey Jude."

And that last meal thing is a rather odd little step in our dance of death, isn't it? You know, for one thing, most executions are scheduled for 12:01 A.M. and, you know, eating that late could really screw up your digestive system.

I also don't understand why we go to such great lengths to protect the well-being of condemned prisoners. From twenty-four-hour suicide watches to the alcohol swab before the lethal injection, time, money, and effort are spent trying to keep these inmates healthy enough to execute. Why? The one thing I would afford these people is the opportunity to give us all a break and off themselves. We ought to decorate their cell with every sharp object known to man, make the bed with preknotted sheets, and place a footstool directly under a strong pipe. I say we put them all in a thirtieth-floor cell with an open window and a bull's-eye painted on the concrete below.

Hey, capital punishment is not about deterrence. We have the police for that. Capital punishment is and always will be about one thing and one thing only: vengeance.

Whether we want to admit it or not, one of the basic characteristics bundled into 99.9 percent of us is a deeply embedded appetite for paybacks. And I believe the people who deny this, who actually maintain that we can evolve to a higher plane, are missing the point. The next step in our evolution should be recognizing the fact that no matter how many eons we place between ourselves and our cave dweller kin, at the core we're just a bunch of primates with beepers looking to crush those who threaten us with a fibula bone left behind at the mud pit. It's time to get back to our primal roots. And I'm willing to do that by accepting the limitations of my species and, when necessary, seeking retribution. Sure, it would be nice if I didn't have to, but it would also be nice if I could flutter my arms and fly.

If you think we take capital punishment too far in the United States, don't spit on the sidewalk with your shoelace untied in Singapore.

There are many countries where the only appeal you get is when you ask the guy with the scimitar to make it snappy. China is to capital punishment what France is to wine. The Chinese will execute you for taking a hit in blackjack on sixteen.

Yeah, I'll tell you the real problem with executions in this country: They just don't sparkle anymore. They need more pizzazz. And if we are going to make capital punishment a spectacle, I say we go all out. Put it on pay per view and give the money to the victims' families. Tostitos presents *The Menendez Brothers' Razzle-Dazzle Tag Team Snuff-orama.*

You know, if it were up to me, I'd bring back some of capital punishment's pomp and mystery. Make the executioner wear a hood. Get rid of the fluorescent lights, give the death chamber that moody, Susan Hayward *I Want to Live!* lighting.

Bring back beheadings, hangings, the firing squad. If you're gonna do it, do it right. And for Christ's sake, the guy's about to pop his clogs, let him have a cigarette. After all, if you're in Florida in the electric chair, there's a good chance that there's going to be plenty of secondhand smoke in the room anyway.

And finally I say we appoint a Secretary of Death. And I would like to personally nominate Jack Kevorkian to be in charge of executions in this country. Yeah. Forget the chair. Good old Dr. Special K can get the job done with a leaf blower, a pool hose, and a smile.

Of course, that's just my opinion, I could be wrong.

Neighbors

Now, I don't want to get off on a rant here, but it hit me yesterday as I found myself in the front yard in my Josie and the Pussie Cats boxer shorts yelling at those damn Fliegelman kids to get the hell off my damn lawn and keep their damn freaky music down, that I am a neighbor.

Aside from your family, no one has more power to hit your buttons than your neighbors. The fact that they live so close to you means they can affect your mood faster than a ladle full of the fruit punch at a techno-rave.

To my way of thinking, neighbors are like hair plugs: The less you notice them, the better they are.

Now, when I say neighbors, I'm talking about the people in your immediate vicinity. I have many wonderful friends in my neighborhood, but it seems like tensions run higher with the folks you directly abut. That's why scouting out the Joneses should be part of the house-buying checklist. How stupid will you feel after signing the deed to your personal Shangri-la, only to arrive home just in time to see your neighbor's boy Mongo pulling up on his no-muffler dirt bike that sounds like an Uzi being fired at a gong?

Now, on a scale of neighborliness where one end is Ned Flanders and the other is Michael Keaton's character in *Pacific Heights,* I fall somewhere in the middle. I've never sat in a dunking chair for the good of a canned food drive, but then again, I've never been arrested for running an unlicensed gator farm out of my crystal meth lab.

But if there is a neighborhood bone of contention about me, it would have to be my fence. While it's true that the fence around my home is sixty feet high, in deference to my neighbors and at great expense to me, it has been expertly painted with a lovely re-creation of exactly what their view was before I built the fence, which includes me, jumping on a trampoline while wearing nothing but a sombrero.

Neighborly relationships take on many forms. In urban environments, say New York City, the first time you learn your neighbor's name is when you see it on the body bag he's being carried out in. Only in New York is "Shut the fuck up, some of us work in the morning" considered a Christmas carol.

Of course, there is an especially dank little corner of Hell in New York that's known as apartment dwelling, where home sweet home is a cramped, poorly ventilated sarcophagus with a subatomic particle's thickness worth of wall separating you from the John Waters casting call of assorted freaks surrounding you on all four sides. You are an unwilling party to your neighbors' most depraved intimacies and Albee-esque dustups as well as conversations that make you wonder if they've got a pet mouse named Algernon.

My New York neighbors were newlyweds. And while they were a sweet, innocent-looking yuppie couple whenever I saw them in the hall, as soon as they shut their balsa wood door behind them, she turned into an insatiably nymphomaniacal Joanne Worley with a cupboard-shaking orgasmic honk that sounded like a migrating goose hooked up to a Peavey thousand-watt amplifier.

And when the husband, whom I came to know as Thor, the human jackhammer, would Sonny Corleone her up against the wall, their headboard would bang so loudly, I would rent action movies and pretend I had Sensurround.

The key to successfully dealing with neighbor problems is simple, I call it the two C's: communication and compromise. For example, I've given all of my neighbors blaze orange hats to wear whenever they are outside their homes so that the guards manning my perimeter towers of the Miller compound don't mistake them for prowlers and accidentally take them out. As you might expect, some of my neighbors are taking exception to this. I can understand that, so I've contracted with a designer to conjure up three distinctive styles of iridescent chapeaux *à l'orange*, at least one of which even the most obstinate neighbor is bound to feel just divine in—especially when they find out that extra hats for visiting friends and relatives are available at cost.

Now this is just one solution. But invariably, the first step toward neighborhood recovery is knowing if you are a bad neighbor. Here are some signs that you just might be:

1. Mr. Rogers files a restraining order against you.

2. The production crew from "Cops" forward all their calls to your house.

3. Your Christmas lights have been up since Christ was born.

And 4. You let your schnauzer shit on your neighbor's lawn so frequently that the dog begins to knock on his door and ask him for reading material.

So if you do have serious problems with a neighbor, here's a great way to deal with it. Don't scream at him; give him a gift.

Go out and buy him the same exact TV that you have. Wrap it up in a big box with a nice ribbon and leave it on his doorstep. Then go home and point your remote out the window at his TV and let the games begin.

Of course, that's just my opinion, I could be wrong.

Country Music

You know who's good on that "Celebrity Jeopardy"? Jeff Foxworthy. Yeah. He kinda surprises you because he plays a country rube for a living, but he's actually a very sharp guy. And very of the moment. Because, as anybody who has ever tuned in to Jerry Springer or watched a Clinton press conference knows, it's a country music world, and those of us who don't accessorize our wardrobe with the Bedazzler, well, just live in it.

Now, I don't want to get off on a rant here, but up until a few years ago it was easy for sneering, cappuccino-toting, urban faux hipsters . . . like me . . . to dismiss country music as the calling card of an alien and somewhat inferior culture which also incorporated protofascist line dancers goose-stepping to a masterwork of musical complexity like "Achy Breaky Heart." But country music has recently experienced an upsurge in popularity that's positively Viagran.

No longer the exclusive domain of big-haired women and men with two first names, it has become as sleek and inescapable a part of the mainstream as the Nike swoosh.

Now, when it comes to country music, I've become as prejudiced as some of the people who listen to it.

Even so, I prefer not to judge another man's music until I've walked a mile in his shoeless, webbed feet.

Why do people love country music? Well, it's a way of blowing off steam over what's bad about life, a means of purging our troubles by setting them to music. Basically, it's this show if I wore bib overalls and said "Yee-haw" instead of "Fuck."

There are many types of country music. There is *trucker* country that is played when you are getting your ass kicked in a truck stop.

There's *cowboy* country where you are getting your ass kicked by guys in ten-gallon hats; there's *hillbilly* country where you're getting your ass kicked by guys with no teeth; and there's *folk* country where you are getting your ass kicked by a lesbian from Saskatchewan.

Now I myself am not a huge fan of any of these forms. I find country music to be a bit simplistic. But while I might be nonplussed by the genre, the typical country music listener is not. God knows, he might not be able to tell you where he was when Kennedy got shot, but he sure as hell knows what two different colored socks he had on the day Billy Joe McCallister jumped off the Tallahatchee Bridge.

And the vortex of that fan base is Branson, Missouri, ground zero for zeros. It's the place where plastic pink flamingos migrate for the winter. Branson is for people who think Graceland isn't quite tacky enough.

Now, I could never go to Branson. There are times I can listen to country music. But I would have a hard time actually watching a show because some of these guys, like Garth Brooks, are wearing jeans so tight that if they tried to squeeze another credit card into their wallets, their dicks would vaporize. Garth Brooks's grafted-on Wranglers make Tom Jones's polyester pelvic tube sock look like a muumuu. Then there's the belt buckles. Christ, these things contain more metal than my grandmother's hip. I've seen belt buckles that big in England, but they serve tea on them.

And back to Garth Brooks for a second. He is officially the biggest ticket seller in the world. The world, folks. That's how far out of the lasso I am. If somebody tells me they're going to watch Garth tonight, I automatically assume they're renting *Wayne's World*.

So while there's a lot of things about country music that I have a quibble with, there is one ingredient in the critter stew that I do find especially succulent: That would be, of course, the song titles. I want to be the guy who sits around all day coming up with little rhinestone gems like:

"Your Momma Might Be a Bad Woman, but She's the Only Sister I Got."

Or "Hand Me the Pool Cue, Then Call Yourself an Ambulance."

"Tell the Dog to Look Away."

"I Hate You More Than Books."

"My Heart's Burning Like a Cross for You."

Or finally, "Honey, You'd Be History If My Tractor Just Had Tits."

Of course, that's just my opinion, I could be wrong.

One Hundred Shows

As originally aired on 5/8/98

Now, I don't want to get off on a rant here, but when we first began this show, nobody believed a guy just talking into a camera would last. But thirty-two directors, 3,456 writers, and four colonoscopies later here I am. Still standing.

So this is the one hundredth show. One hundred times I've stood on this stage and rifled through the attaché case of discontent that is permanently handcuffed to my brain stem.

And you know what else a hundred shows represents? A lot of "fucks." I say the word "fuck" more often than Jake La Motta being Rolfed. In fact, I'll let you in on a secret.

HBO pays me by the "fuck." Fuck fuck fuck. I just paid for my kids' college. Fuck fuck fuck fuck fuck. There's a boat. Fuck fuck fuckity-fuck fuck fuck. Those were just for me.

You know, in all the hoopla surrounding my one hundredth episode haven't we all lost sight of something? You know, "Seinfeld"'s last show is less than a week away. Please, people, please, forget about me. Can't we let Jerry have his moment?

Now, of course, the only way I can do this twenty-seven-minute show once a week, twenty-six weeks a year, with only a week off every four shows, is with the support of my wife and two children. Thank you for being there, honey. I'm truly the luckiest little pirate in all of Puppetland.

My favorite part of the show has to be the rant. I go through each rant with so much attention and care, there's none left when I go to choose my movie roles.

You see, this camera . . . is my own personal soapbox that lets me vent about the important issues of our day. Like driving in my car yesterday, I jotted down an observation. I wrote it on this napkin. I don't know, let's see, it says: DO SOMETHING ABOUT STUPID BUMPER STICKERS. You see, that's the joy of doing this show. Taking on the big guys.

Now, tonight I'd like to clear up some misconceptions some of you have about the show. People always ask me how many newspapers do I have to read every day to come up with all those jokes? Well, I usually start at 2 A.M. with the wire service from Hong Kong and work my way through the morning editions of the East Coast papers, and then finish it up around 8 P.M. with the *International Herald Tribune.* In other words, I read "Beetle Bailey" once a week and occasionally take a stab at the "Jumble."

Honestly, a huge part of the success of this show is the writing. We've won a couple of awards for that and I really want to congratulate all my writers by name. Problem is, I'm so detached from the inner workings of this show, I don't know their names.

So whoever wrote this for me, thank you. You bald losers.

I'd also like to thank the little people. Specifically, Willie and Keno, the two midgets who operate the life-sized Dennis Miller animatronic puppet that you see before you. I'm actually at home right now in my undies scratching my ass with a melon scoop. I haven't been here since show fourteen.

Now, wardrobe is a very important component of this program, the impact of which cannot be overstated. If you only knew how much care I take in making sure that I always borrow pants from a stagehand who is nearly my size.

Now, I know that there are a lot of people who feel that once you've tasted success and achieved a modicum of material comfort, you go soft and lose your edge. Well, I'm living proof that nothing could be further from the truth. From the time I get up in the morning to berate my game-keeper Kang for overfeeding the peacocks to later that evening when I select my handmade silken ascot for that evening's postprandial harpsichord recital, my mind is constantly teeming with satiric rage about life's injustices. Because I'm still what I always was . . . Sir Joseph Six-Pack the Third.

But in all seriousness, if there's one regret I have about the show over the years, it's that somewhere along the way I might have hurt somebody's feelings. I know most people don't realize this, but all I want to do is make a point, puncture a little pomposity, and get a laugh without ever really hurting anyone.

That's actually the hardest part of the job, driving home from a show at night and thinking, "Hey, why did I have to say that?" So if during the past one hundred episodes I may have hurt your feelings, well, blow me.

Of course, that's just my opinion, I could be wrong.

The Republican Party

Now, I don't want to get off on a rant here, but you know, maybe the reason Republicans are so pro-gun is because they need them to constantly shoot themselves in the foot.

It has been nearly seven years since Newt Gingrich and his band of fascist elves stormed Capitol Hill promising to toss out the old to make room for something even older: greed and fear.

Then, right around the time Clinton and Newt were duking it out over the budget and opening and shutting the federal government like bedroom doors in a Richard Lester movie, the American public began to realize that some of the Congressional Class of '94's ideas were about as humane as running the Iditarod with a team of Taco Bell Chihuahuas pulling the sled.

We listened to this Republican Congress shrieking for two years like the colicky baby of Lou Costello and Bjork about campaign finance reforms only to see them fizzle like charcoal briquettes at a fraternity beer bash. Well, how did that happen?

Oh yeah, didn't I read something about Newt Gingrich receiving illegal campaign contributions? Naw, that would be too perfect. That would be like saying that the nation's most vocal proponent of family values had an affair with another woman while his wife was on her deathbed . . . Never mind.

Former Speaker Newt Gingrich sums up the Republicans' problems in a nutcase. Their most extreme members are more out of step with the rest of America than Joe Cocker in a line dance. Remember, this is the party of Strom Thurmond and Jesse Helms, men so stiff they make Herman Munster look like Alvin Ailey.

The classic, distilled philosophical difference between Republicans and Democrats has always been about the ideal size and scope of government. Republicans say that Democrats want a huge monolithic federal institution that will compromise personal liberty and freedom by controlling individuals' lives with intrusive policies and a dictatorial agenda. Republicans, of course, believe that is the job of organized religion.

In the end, partisan politics is what it needs to be, a constant tug-o-war anchored by the fattest white asses on each side. So as Newt Gingrich, Trent Lott, and Dick Armey dig their tassel-loafered heels into the muck and strain with all their might to move the weight of public opinion in their favor, old Bill's got his end tied up to the hitch of a Mardi Gras float and he's sitting in a La-Z-Boy with a corn dog, waving to people while Miss Nude America rubs blueberry hot lube into his fleshy shoulders.

And that's because the one thing Clinton has going for him is compassion. And you're about as likely to find a Republican who's connected to the needs of women, minorities, and the poor as you are a naked chick silhouetted on a mud flap in the parking lot of the Lilith Fair.

You know, God has no place in politics. Quite frankly, if God saw the way some Republicans invoked His name, He'd turn atheist.

But you've got to feel sorry for the Republicans. They're constantly painting fake tunnels on the sides of cliff walls, only to see President Clinton somehow beep beep right through them.

See, Clinton is like the bad guy in *Terminator 2: Judgment Day;* able to assume the shape and voice of his enemies to get what he needs. He appropriated Republican ideas, added a little dash of his inimitable dewy-eyed "Bubba" magic, and presto! The next thing you know, ol' Jed's a millionaire.

The Republicans had no idea of who they were going up against when they took on Clinton. And as any intern who's ever encountered the President in a West Wing hallway can tell you, Clinton does his best work when his back is to the wall.

The Republicans need to stop taking themselves so seriously, pull the American flagpole out of their ass, and lighten the fuck up.

Of course, that's just my opinion, I could be wrong.

The Extinction of Customer Service

Customer service has gone the way of the paddle wheel and the nickel blowjob. Those were heady days.

Now, I don't want to get off on a rant here, but trying to find the customer service counter in a department store in 1998 America is like trying to find a clock in a casino.

Between the catatonic indifference and the Nurse Ratched–like attitudes, you have a better chance of winning the Publishers Clearing House Sweepstakes, finding the Holy Grail in your garage and the lost city of Atlantis in your septic tank all in the same day than you do of finding one goddamn human being out there who can help you with anything.

I mean, doesn't it seem like the frail consumer seated on the supply and demand seesaw is more and more frequently being catapulted into oblivion by the big fat ass of corporate incompetence?

One main reason for the nosedive in efficient service is the stupidification of America. In the name of quick cash, many businesses have cut their costs by replacing career-minded professionals with lukewarm bodies so close to flatlining they might as well be wearing their name tags on their toes.

And nowadays, many companies are getting smart and putting their employees who don't speak English on the front lines of the consumer service battle. That's fine with me. I love it.

I like to bring my family and watch the show as the customer in line in front of me tries to explain to Kipchogi, who's fresh off the hovercraft from Nepal, just what went wrong with his VCR, or as Kip refers to it, the "magic story box."

You know, personally, I believe the Devil himself hand-picked his own favorite children to work in the retail field. Now, granted, I understand that long hours, truculent customers, and lousy pay are as much a part of the job as refolding the same fucking sweater for eight hours. But if you don't like it, go back to school and find another job, but don't take it out on me. It's not my fault that you're fighting with your boyfriend Werner von Methlab or your newly pierced nipple is throbbing, or Heather brought you a latté when you specifically asked for a decaf mocha. I just need a new pair of chinos, Cruella?

And the absolute nexus—Christ, I feel like Gene Roddenberry—the absolute nexus of customer service is the computer industry. You're put on hold longer than Ralph Macchio's career, while listening to a Muzak version of *Cheap Trick Live at Budokan,* and when you finally get through, you either get a precocious nine-year-old whose primary qualification for the job is an exhaustive knowledge of Lara Croft from *Tomb Raider II*'s bra size, or an embittered Mountain Dew-aholic who is so burnt out from dealing with cybermorons all day that he can't abide your particular techno-impotence. Well, I'm sorry, but if you're going to take an intricate labyrinth of circuitry and put it on store shelves at the Price Club next to the fruit dehydrators, you'd damn well better be helpful and informative when you get a frantic phone call from some Luddite whose greatest prior technological achievement was Xeroxing his ass. Okay?

Let's face it, when you encounter poor customer service, your options are limited. The classic course of action is to ask for a supervisor. You want to know my theory? There are no supervisors. There are only two people in the room and the imbecile you're talking to and his imbecile buddy take turns pretending to be the supervisor.

Anyway, corporate America has shown its hand and said all it cares about is the bottom line. It cares nothing about customer service or its employees and, as a matter of fact, by shipping jobs overseas, it shows it cares nothing about our country. So when its products don't work, cut it no slack because it cuts us none. You want to make sneakers in a converted reconnaissance tunnel somewhere under the Mekong Delta by embryos earning three cents a year?

Well, they better be good sneakers, or else I'm returning them, motherfucker, and no, I don't have the receipt. Okay?

Of course, that's just my opinion, I could be wrong.

Apathy & Cynicism

Now, I don't want to get off on a rant here, but apathy and cynicism have become so rampant in America that the motto on our coins should be changed from *E Pluribus Unum* to "Yeah, right."

Sure, many of you might assume that I would include myself among the naysayers. Well, you'd be wrong. As a matter of fact, I'm so optimistic that for years now I've had to put on this curmudgeon act to keep from spontaneously bursting into tears of joy. No kidding, people who know me well actually have a nickname for me, "Dappy," which is an amalgam of "Dennis" and "happy." Dappy!

Truth be told, I'm actually equal parts cynicism and apathy. I'm always willing to believe the worst as long as it doesn't take too much effort.

I believe that every cloud, every dark cloud has a silver lining that contains abnormally high traces of mercury, which will eventually lead to the onset of neurological disorder.

But that's me. What I don't understand is that there's no reason for society to be moping around like a grounded teenager. I mean, we're not at war, there's no rioting, and the Spice Girls are in their fourteenth minute, you know . . . Face facts, our economy is on methamphetamine, for Christ's sake. We should be bouncing up and down like those jumpsuit freaks in the Pentium van. Instead, I keep expecting to turn on PBS and catch Barney singing "My Name Is Luka."

And of course, the B-side of this never-ending song of futility is apathy, which feeds like a suckbird on cynicism's bloated carcass. You know, much like Hitchcock's film cameos, I like to weave the phrase "suckbird on cynicism's bloated carcass" into each one of my rants. Sort of like Hirschfeld's "Ninas." But I digress . . . I digress like a suckbird on cynicism's bloated carcass.

Now, there's one specific area in which a skeptical frame of mind is a completely necessary and indispensable defense mechanism, an indestructible umbrella against a raging shitstorm called politics. Politics rightfully earns our cynicism and apathy. For many of us, Watergate took our maidenhead, and ever since then we've wondered if it's the cream that rises to the top or something else you see floating around in porcelain bowls.

We are skeptical of our government because we have weathered so many scandals in the past thirty years we don't expect anything different from the people we elect. As long as the economy is sound, you can fuck us all you want, just make sure you leave the money on the dresser when you leave.

And trying to change politics is like trying to turn off "Wheel of Fortune" at the day room of a senior citizens' center. Somewhere along the line, you're gonna catch a urine bag upside the head.

People have become cynical in their jobs as well because of downsizing. You don't believe your boss anymore when he tells you you're part of the family. Your family doesn't move to Brazil and replace you with a cheaper brother.

And many other institutions we once held in high esteem have opened themselves up to disdain. I don't know about you, but ever since O.J. walked out of that courtroom and into the loving arms of his caddie, my esteem for the judicial system has plummeted like Roger Ebert on a bungee cord. And the only deliberation Terry Nichols's jury should've had is which arm to put the needle in. And didn't we all hear the blind lady holding the scales of justice say "What the fuck" when that scumbag British nanny skated away?

The twentieth century has kicked us in the teeth so repeatedly we could headline at the Grand Ol' Opry. First, Einstein proved that reality itself makes less sense than Rod Steiger's dream journal. Then, in short order, we got the atomic bomb, the Cold War, the McCarthy hearings, John met Yoko, and then we discovered that "The Flintstones" was not, in fact, filmed before a live studio audience. Is it any wonder we all started turning off our hearing aids?

So what's the electric snake going to be that will rooter out the apathy-clogged drain of the American spirit? Hope. You know what gives me hope? Knowing that we human beings all have the power to change. Take my old college roommate, Todd. He must have weighed four hundred pounds. Plus he was a Quaalude freak, an alcoholic. I saw him today after about fifteen years. And you know something . . . still weighs four hundred pounds, and he was drunk on his ass, high as a kite, but, God bless him, he's a woman now.

And so, too, we all must change. Our wide-eyed sense of wonder should no longer be reserved exclusively for Ron Popeil's pasta maker . . . although she's a real honey, ain't she? Just as a common courtesy to each other, maybe we should all pledge to wait until February first before we give up on the New Year.

Of course, that's just my opinion, I could be wrong.

The War on Drugs

Now, I don't want to get off on a rant here, but America's war on drugs has turned out to be as fruitless as Pavarotti's diet. We seem to be fighting this multifront campaign with all the cool-headed expertise of the Three Stooges fixing a leaky faucet.

And how can we say we're serious about eradicating drugs when there's actually a twenty-four-hour TV network in this country that broadcasts nothing but cartoons?

Christ, you could not keep a straight face about our drug policy if you were David Brinkley on a Vicodin drip.

I mean, when you think about it, who really is fighting this supposed war on drugs? Let's face it, folks, we have a couple of "McHale's Navy" boats, four dogs who got tired of sniffing other dogs' asses, and that commercial with the eggs. And that is it. Okay?

The war on drugs is nothing more than a syringe full of platitudes that politicians try to mainline into the public's happy vein to keep us compliant. If we had any actual commitment, you'd be able to look at a map and see a smoking hole where Colombia once was. Short of that, the war on drugs has failed. Oh wait. I take that back, my kid got thrown out of school this week because they caught him with some menthol-flavored Ricolas.

The war on drugs is a farce, and here's why: Getting high is hard-wired into our DNA. It's a basic human need right up there with food, clothing, and "Seinfeld." Ever since primitive man first looked around the crude lean-to he'd built and thought, "Man, I need an escape from this Arthur C. Clarke shithole," then loaded some mastodon dung into a bongasaurus and proceeded to get so swacked that he would order a slab of ribs that could literally tip his car over, people have used any and all means at their disposal to alter their perception of reality.

Look, we can't just point our fingers at the drug-producing nations and whine about their lawlessness and disregard for human life, because we're inextricably entwined with them in a lock-step tango of supply and demand. We comprise 5 percent of the planet's population and consume 50 percent of the planet's illicit drugs. I got that off the liner notes for *Yessongs*.

We may complain about the neighbors, but we're rummaging through their medicine cabinet like Gary Busey's babysitter every chance we get. We need to get the mirror off the coffee table and take a long, hard look at ourselves without giggling and realize that our attitude toward drugs is more conflicted than Woody Allen at a family reunion.

Now, I myself don't do drugs, because as I grew older, I began to discover that they're not nearly powerful enough to quell my exquisite inner pain.

But even I believe that at the very least, marijuana should be available to those who need it for medical reasons. And no, going to see the director's cut of *Blade Runner* is not a medical reason. *Showgirls*, maybe.

Look, the role of government is to protect us from other nations and other people; the government has no business protecting me from me.

But we refuse to accept that you can't save someone who doesn't want to be saved. I have come to the realization that America doesn't have a drug problem, *some* Americans do. And it is their personal responsibility to fix it, not mine. Their drug problem only becomes my problem when they operate a moving vehicle, try to sell drugs to a minor, or corner me at a party and try to explain to me who really killed Bruce Lee.

If a fully grown adult in reasonable control of his faculties wants to plunge a syringe full of lighter fluid into his urethra and piss fire, as long as he does it in the privacy of his own asbestos bathroom, I will flick the Bic.

We need to face the facts. What we're doing isn't working because we don't really believe in it, and achieving any kind of tangible victory in this wishy-washy Vietnam-like quagmire is like trying to fuck a woman while she's still wearing her pantyhose.

Our leaders need to ease up on the *Go Ask Alice* knee-jerk hysteria and come up with some real solutions. Like reconfigure the molecular structure of cocaine so it makes people fat. Or more seriously, I say we legalize drugs. Strip them of their outlaw glamour so kids aren't as attracted to them, regulate their price so they're no longer a viable commodity for the disenfranchised, tax the shit out of them and give us all a kickback that we can then spend on cigarettes, booze, and coffee.

Hey . . . Let's face it, folks, drugs aren't going anywhere, America. Any substance that helps ugly guys get laid is here to stay.

Of course, that's just my opinion, I could be wrong.

Survival of the Fittest

ow, I don't want to get off on a rant here, but in an era in which able-bodied college football players scam handicapped parking spaces, survival of the fittest has become a win-at-all-costs steel cage Battle Royale in which only the last man standing wins. Unfortunately, many people act as if the rules of decorum are made to be broken . . . if possible, into jagged shards which you can then use to maim your competition.

Hey, anybody who thinks the basic, visceral, territorial instinct to survive through physical aggression died with our knuckle-dragging ancestors hasn't foraged for a Furby in a Toys "R" Us the day before Christmas.

Truth be told, our country wasn't founded by the strongest or the smartest from other countries, but by those who dared to take a risk. They were competitors who wouldn't accept the role their own repressive society assigned them. That's why they came here, because America is the land of unlimited opportunity for all. *Offer not available equally in all fifty states. Some blacks, Jews, women, gays, and Mexicans may not qualify. See your leaders for details.*

The socioeconomic food chain in America is as brutal and impersonal as a cavity search in a Turkish airport. The fight for the corner office, the good table, and the orchestra pit seats is as savage as two beauty contestants fighting over the last of the nipple tape. Nipple tape—another wondrous innovation from your friends at 3M.

You know, personally, I consider myself lucky by Hollywood standards because in my climb up the comedy ladder, I've only had to destroy five, maybe six thousand people. Let's face it, show business is just one big daisy chain of nonstop mean. It is the worst fucking business I never plan to leave.

In purely biological terms, those who survive get to pass on their superior genes to the next generation: Michael lives, Fredo dies. Bill Clinton exposes himself to low-level civil servants, gropes volunteers in the Oval Office, gives skin flute lessons to chunky interns, and skates away like Brian Boitano with a Dexatrim shunt strapped to the inside of his unitard.

Al Gore goes to Vietnam, champions the environment, comes home to the same woman for the last twenty-five or so years, he's in deeper shit than a midget cleaning a Porta-Potty at a bran muffin factory in Mexico.

And even though we're not dwelling in caves anymore and relying on brute strength and hunting skills to keep us fed, survival of the fittest is still alive and well, it's merely adapted itself in order to . . . uhh . . . to survive. Where once the hulking no-necks of the tribe were the ones who flourished, they've been replaced by the uberdweebs—guys like Bill Gates. Let's face it, if Gates had been around in the Stone Age, I guarantee you, he would've spent all his time plucking loincloth wedgies out of his scrawny white buttcrack.

And remember, when we talk about the survival of the fittest, it's all about context. Sure, the lion is the undisputed king of the jungle, but airdrop him into Antarctica, and he's just a penguin's bitch.

Although man is the supreme species, he is still the only animal seemingly at odds with his instinct to survive. Too often it seems we rule over the world reluctantly, as though we did something wrong by being there on top. Hey, the only time a shark second-guesses himself is when he swings on back around because in all that commotion, he forgot to check and see if the surfer had any friends he could munch on, all right?

You know, we shouldn't be uncomfortable with our own power. Even the most accepting of us has, at one time or another, dreamed of establishing a far-reaching eugenics program that would require mandatory sterilization for anyone who wears a beer hat, screams "You da man" at golf tournaments, or drives a car with a NO FAT CHICKS bumper sticker, all right?

Bottom line. Competition is good for the country, good for the economy, and good for the world. But that doesn't mean that we have to ignore our more humane instincts. Because if you're going to live your life solely by the tenet of survival of the fittest, well then, you might as well just start running under the fridge every time the kitchen light comes on, okay?

But just as necessary as compassion for the weak is measured respect for the strong. Instead of resenting the adept, the more talented, the great-looking, the rich, the painfully charismatic, isn't it really better to step back and be grateful that they're here among us? Too often, losers don't know they are losers. So listen to me. Think of Harrison Ford . . . You . . . You . . . Harrison Ford . . . You get it? Don't you feel better now that you know your place in the cosmic order, because you can bet your ass Harrison Ford does, my friends.

Of course, that's just my opinion, I could be wrong.

Aging Gracefully

ow, I don't want to get off on a rant here, but getting old is a relative concept. A mayfly is old after twelve hours. A cat is old in ten years. And Ricky Martin Fever is old as of . . . uh . . . right about now.

The difficulty of aging gracefully is that there are so few examples of it in popular culture. Any book, movie, or TV program geared toward older folks stands out like Marty Feldman in a Beijing police lineup. Aside from the occasional *Diagnosis Murder*, advertisers are after the fourteen to thirty demographic. Why? Because older people don't tolerate stupid shit as much as young people do. You never see an eighty-year-old geek camping out in front of the local movie theater dressed as his favorite character from a Merchant/Ivory film. All right?

What frightens me most about getting old? I guess it's the thought of my first gray pubic hair, because if there's one thing I'm proud of, it's my thick, luxuriant, chestnut brown bush.

I never think of myself as being old because my work in television keeps me young. Do you realize Mike Wallace of "60 Minutes" is over eighty years old? Think Mike likes the sound of that ticking stopwatch in the background every week?

You know, I love it when old people reach the point in their lives when they just don't give a shit and will say anything to anybody, anytime. It's like senior Tourette's or something. I got an uncle who's about ninety years old and he answers the phone: "Bite me, you beady-eyed baboon fucker."

Even sex doesn't have to end now that you are older. With Viagra you can get harder than your arteries and have a great sex life. But I fear we might find out the problems with Viagra somewhere down the line. How did the entire medical establishment forget that a man cannot pee with an erection? You give an eighty-year-old guy an eight-hour chubby, he's going to make the *Hindenburg* explosion look like one of Jiminy Cricket's farts.

Since hopefully all of us will take the final victory lap in life's marathon, here are some tips on how to make things easier for all of us as you grow older:

You know that story about how you could've bought the entire San Fernando Valley for $250 back in 1938? Well, we've heard it. Okay? Maybe six or seven thousand times. Now get on the ice floe. Bye-bye now.

Also, old people, stick to eating the early bird special before 5 P.M., so those of us born in this millennium can eat dinner without having our waitress go on sabbatical for forty-five minutes at a time so she can assure Gramps Muldoon that yes, the navy bean soup indeed has to come with beans in it.

And lastly, just buy the fruit. All right? Some of these old guys go over the produce like they're Orson Welles picking out blouses for Ruth Warrick in *Citizen Kane*. It's fruit. Okay? For Christ's sake, I'm trying to get through the line, and I got an Easter Island statue in front of me running a carbon 14 test on a fucking cling peach. Can I go home now, pappy?

You know, it'll be interesting to see how Bill Clinton ages. He's definitely not going to acquire any dignity or depth with his advancing years. Face it, he'll never be the grand old man of the Democratic Party.

I see Clinton as one of those old guys on the boardwalk in Atlantic City, with skin the color of beef jerky and all this white cotton candy chest hair, clad in a red Speedo, black knee-high socks and sandals, and wearing enough Paco Rabanne to gag a Brazilian pimp, standing there making kissy-kissy sounds whenever a woman who's not attached to an oxygen canister walks by.

Hey, you know, folks, aging is a constant process that only stops when we do. We should welcome the wisdom that comes with experience, but instead we waste our dwindling energies combating the exterior signs of aging, spending countless dollars and hours in a futile and desperate attempt to look like something we're not. I say, turn in the direction of the skid, people. Guys, be proud when you hike the waistband of those kelly green Sansabelt slacks that you mail-ordered from *Parade* magazine up around the nipple level, all right? Ladies, don't let anybody tell you that Slurpee blue isn't a great color for human hair. And everybody, clack those dentures like you're Lord of the Dance having a fucking seizure. It is all good. Okay?

Except for one thing and one thing only. You've got to change your driving habits. First of all, it would help everyone's confidence level if you wore an expression on your face that said something other than "I have zero peripheral vision, and we're all going to crash and die!"

And most importantly, if you're doing twelve miles an hour in the fast lane of the 405, well then, you gotta pick it up, man, 'cause, if time is of the essence for anyone, it's you, Mr. Meet Joe Black. So let's go! Go! Go! Go! Go! Go! Go!

Of course, that's just my opinion, I could be wrong.

Our Overdependence on Technology/Y2K Bug

Now, I don't want to get off on a rant here, but information is flying at us faster than bullshit at a White House press briefing, and keeping abreast of it all is harder than getting Siamese twins into a kayak. Sorry, I'm officially out of similes.

We've become dependent on the computer for so many things lately—shopping, entertainment, information, masturbation—that I simply can't imagine my life without it. How would I get through the day knowing that I could no longer troll the Internet for hours at a time, stopping only to sip from the flagon of knowledge that is Harvey Korman's autobiography?

Or reading what some Yahoo!-surfing yahoo thinks about the hidden messages contained in the opening credits of "The X-Files"? Christ, I hope Duchovny's making enough money to build a really, really big fence.

Well, here's the latest skinny. Come January 1, the shit will supposedly interface with the fan because most computers won't be able to recognize the year 2000 if it walks up and megabytes them on the ass. Uh-huh. So what's the big deal? You're saying the genius at 7-Eleven won't be able to open the cash drawer? Yeah. Like he can do that now.

But I guess for some people, maybe this will be a disaster. Because let's face it, the average American is so enamored of high-tech toys that he makes Inspector Gadget look like an Amish elder in a power outage. And while I can see some of the techno-attraction, there are certain places where I draw the line in the silicon sand.

One thing which I do not entrust to technology at all is my show. Since it bears my name, I feel an obligation to present you, the viewer, with entertainment that's painstakingly hand-crafted. All our jokes are lovingly slow-brewed in small batches according to a secret formula that's been handed down through generations of smugmasters. And every rant is written on parchment in ink made from berries grown and hand-gathered by monks who live, work and pray in the "Dennis Miller Live" Franciscan seminary located in the basement of my studio.

You know, I think I would buy into this Y2K disaster thing a lot more if the survivalist subculture hadn't cried

Apocalypse at every other out-of-the-ordinary occurrence in our lifetime from the comet Kahoutek to the discovery of a yam shaped like Morley Safer.

And you know something? If the nutsos are right and the only people who will survive are those nuts who stockpile guns, Bibles, and a year's supply of Mrs. T's pierogies and Bosco, well, I think I'd rather punch out with the cool kids, 'cause if my only option is sharin' some jerky with Bob Barr and drinking my own recycled whiz, well, I'll take my chances in Thunderdome, okay?

And I have a little problem with the idea of spending nearly a trillion dollars to solve this thing. How's about just taking your computer back to the kid at Circuit City who sold it to you and saying, "Hey, you stuck me with a machine with a broken clock. Now fix it, asshole."

So why is it, with all the computer geniuses out there, solutions to the Y2K problem are scarcer than J. D. Salinger appearances on "Hollywood Squares"?

You mean to tell me in the entire computer industry, there was not one nearsighted geek farsighted enough to take a few minutes away from designing the blood spatter pattern on Duke Nukem to teach their machine how to fucking count? Come on, guys, get on the joystick. It's not like you have *lives* to go home to, all right? I guess we shouldn't be surprised that these cybereunuchs don't know how to handle a date.

Look, while catastrophe is unlikely, there's gonna be some glitches. If there's a widespread breakdown of computer networks, you won't have access to your ATM, you won't be able to talk on a cell phone or program your VCR, and you won't be able to buy gas for your car. My God, Mr. Peabody . . . in the blink of an eye, we'll be catapulted all the way back to 1977! Damn you, Y2K bug! Damn you to hell!

Folks, let's bottom-line this. The Millennial Gloomy Guses are telling us that the collapse of Western Civilization is going to be brought about by *two missing digits,* and I just can't buy that. It's like saying basketball's going to lose its fan base 'cause one guy retires. Okay, bad example. It's like saying the presidency is going to be brought down by a simple blow . . . Okay, worse example. It's like saying—oh hell. You know what? We're all gonna fucking die.

Of course, that's just my opinion, I could be wrong.

Faith

Now, I don't want to get off on a rant here, but what is faith? Well, essentially, faith is the voice in the back of your head that tells you to listen to the voice in the back of your head.

People are looking toward the heavens for answers these days because quite frankly, down here on Planet Bottom Line, the only answer you'll get to your spiritual questions is "Do that on your own time, freak." Okay?

We are desperate to find something to believe in. That's why Bill Clinton is doing so well; we don't give a damn if we can *believe* him, as long as we can believe in him . . . Do me a favor and don't think about that too much or it's going to seem a lot less clever.

Now, as for me, I've chosen bits and pieces of the standard religious fare served up during my formative years and tailored it to meet my own needs. For example, when I was thirteen years old, I really did believe that idle hands were the Devil's workshop, so I was constantly jerking off.

Listen, I'm the first one to admit that I'm somewhat cynical when it comes to faith. I envy people who can just let go and totally commit. I, on the other hand, can't even hear the title of the show "Touched by an Angel" without thinking that a professional baseball player is being sued for sexual harassment.

But the thing that bothers me most is fake faith. Some performers say a prayer before they step onstage and I can't think of anything more narcissistic. Does Madonna really think that with all the hunger and strife in this world, God can spare a nanosecond worrying whether or not her dancers Javier and Lance mistimed their jetés during "Papa Don't Preach"?

I guess if I ever do get to meet my maker, the first question I'd have to ask Him is what's up with the hair in the armpits? And why does it feel so good when I rub my eyes real hard? And why did you give us animals that we have to pet but no animals that pet us? And I'm not talking about the dog licking the apple sauce off my thingy because the only reason he does that is because he wants the apple sauce. I'm talking about an animal who pets us for the sole reason of seeing us smile.

Hey, it's great to have faith, but come on, temper it with a little good old-fashioned earthbound smarts. I mean if you're a Christian Scientist hemophiliac, don't even think about getting a job as an assistant to a walleyed knife thrower. Saw that on a card at Spencers Gifts.

Now, once you get a few folks to share in your faith, you got yourself a religion. As the Bible says: "Where two or more are gathered, you can take up a collection."

I guess the thing I find strange about most religions and going to church is the church itself. I don't get it. Doesn't the existence of an opulent building go against the very foundation it is supposed to be built on? I mean, meet under a tarp and give the money you save on stained glass to build houses for poor people, feed the homeless, or raise the spending cap for the NBA teams.

Look, I think faith is a wonderful thing. If your faith enables you somehow to survive life's shitstorms with a modicum of grace and humor, you are truly blessed. However, if having faith means that you give your kids' college money to some cosmic shyster who wants to borrow your balls so he can go on a comet ride with the Silver Surfer, well, you're just being phenomenally stupid. Okay? And trust me, the real God thinks so too.

Hey, maybe there's a reason we're not handed all the answers in an easy-to-open, Oscar-style envelope. Maybe faith isn't about what's up on top of the mountain; maybe it's about how far we're willing to climb to get there. Maybe we don't know the answers because not knowing makes us better people, forcing us to huddle together for warmth in existential darkness and, in the process, bringing all of us closer together. Or maybe we're just all a bunch of fucking morons.

Now, of course, I don't mean that . . . I'm not a moron . . . and I do have faith. I see the Lord's work every day. A majestic sunrise, the dew on the lawn, my loving wife, my beautiful children, and, of course, witnessing the miracle of the asswipe in the Range Rover that just cut me off being pulled over and cavity searched by the highway patrol.

Of course, that's just my opinion, I could be wrong.

Super Consumers

Now, I don't want to get off on a rant here, but our nation's shopping obsession is rapidly filling our homes with a random array of useless shit that makes Charles Foster Kane's basement look like the inside of Dan Quayle's head. Spendthrift, credit-happy America has a worse case of consumption than any character Charles Dickens ever created.

You know how to tell when you've got a shopping problem? When the lights in the department store momentarily dim after they slide your credit card through the thing.

America's current fiscal strategy is often more out of balance than a drunk guy logrolling with an inner ear infection during Mardis Gras. In the face of supposed political turmoil and worldwide market upheavals, what do an increasing number of us do to assuage our fiscal anxiety? We, of course, go out and spend more money. These days Americans will buy anything they can lay their Oliver Peoples–shaded eyes on, whether it's Foamy, the Rabid Badger Beanie Baby, or

$1,200 Rolling Stones tickets, or the entire International Olympic Committee for that matter.

Basically, my feelings on shallow consumerism can be summed up thusly. I don't think masturbating to the Hammacher Schlemmer catalog is wrong, but the Hickory Farms catalog, that is sick.

Although that Gouda wheel is lookin' mighty purrty.

Personally, I hate shopping. I never know where to begin. Am I an "active gent"? Or "youthfully elegant"? Neither, but I've never seen a men's department section called: LATE, DOUBLE-PARKED, AND PISSED OFF.

I hate the salesperson who thinks you're more likely to buy something from them if they learn your first name and then start beatin' it like a coked-up monkey on a snare drum. Hey, back off with the name, Sam Drucker. You're selling me a shirt, not talking me off a fucking ledge, okay?

People deal with money in different ways. Some people hide their finances from their spouse. I guess that's me because my wife doesn't know I'm doing this show for a living. She thinks I'm the assistant manager at a Sizzler in Ventura and have to work late on Fridays to close out the cash drawer. When she asks me how we can afford such a nice house on my salary, I tell her I sell some of the borderline meat out of the trunk of my car to junkies who don't know any better . . . It's just business.

What drives the American obsession for more? What drives it? More is better than less. Okay? Like if I had seventeen foot massagers from Brookstone, well, if I had eighteen, that would be better. You with me? Eighteen better than seventeen. Critics like to attack the blindly acquisitive nature of the American consumer, but the desire to collect the most nuts is hard-wired into our inner squirrel.

Okay, so we're living for the fleeting pleasures of today and not giving a thought to the bitter realities of the future. So we're all being grasshoppers and not ants. Worst-case scenario? You wind up digging through other people's trash to survive. The way things are going, at least it'll be really nice trash, in matching Louis Vuitton twist-top bags.

I mean, what fun is having money anyway unless you can use it? You know what happens to money you don't spend? It sits in bank accounts and it grows, slowly becoming more money and more money until one day you just die and your next of kin, Cousin Tommy with the plate in his head, converts your 401(k) into singles and starts feeding G-strings at the titty bar next door to the cemetery.

Americans have a guaranteed right to life, liberty, and the pursuit of happiness and if that means the whole country becomes one big giant coast-to-coast shopping mall where the Grand Canyon is the Gap, then I say, "Hey, put me on a burro, point it toward the relaxed-fit khakis, and slap it on the ass."

Of course, that's just my opinion, I could be wrong.

Death of Eccentricity

Come on, haven't we evolved to the point in this culture where carrying a purse doesn't necessarily mean you're gay? Can't it mean you're just eccentric? Well, I guess it could, if eccentricity weren't so prevalent nowadays. I'm beginning to think the norm is now Norm Bates. The real freak is the guy who puts on a tie, goes off to work, does his job, comes home, eats dinner, turns on the TV, and falls asleep in the same bed as his wife . . . Now, that's fuckin' weird!

Now, I don't want to get off on a rant here, but eccentricity is dead. At least that's what I told my friend Mr. Winkles, the chimp that I dress in a tuxedo, who follows me around in a little miniature Porsche squirting people with a seltzer bottle full of his own urine.

At one time in this country's cozy, homogenous, Richie Cunningham past, eccentricity was the exclusive domain of the outcast, the disaffected, and the disenfranchised. Back then, breaking free of the tight behavioral constraints imposed by society was a significantly brave, if not desperate, act.

The problem now is that the bar of abnormality is constantly being ratcheted higher and higher. Oddness has become the coin of the realm. Now everybody wants to be the weird kid, in a calculated attempt to appear talented, deep, different, or, at the very least, fuckable.

Carnival freak shows are going out of business because they can't top the demented pageantry at the local Greyhound bus terminal. I mean, why part with your hard-earned cash to see a hermaphroditic dwarf pound tenpenny nails through his skull when you can just watch a guy in a Hefty bag and hip waders purchase a ticket to Parma, Ohio, with a tube sock full of pennies and a half-eaten braunschweiger sandwich?

Let's face it, computer technology now gives us unlimited access to the bizarre. Ten-year-olds can type "elephantitis" into their Internet search engine and download medical pictures of men with enormous scrotal sacks and turn them into greeting cards that read: YOU'VE GOT A LOT OF BALLS HAVING ANOTHER BIRTHDAY.

It seems that being inundated with the Kaczynskis and the Kato Kalins and Tysons and Tonyas and the Flynts and the Fleisses has opened up a broad spectrum of accepted behavior that ranges from Marilyn Manson to Marilyn Quayle. And the general consensus seems to be it's all good. We have become so blasé we make Robert Wagner look like BeetleJuice.

Now, one of the eccentrics I do respect is Dr. Jack Kevorkian. Lives alone, likes to paint, plays the flute, keeps to himself, and occasionally ventures out of the house to whack a patient. Sure, he's weird. But he's not hurting anybody.

And for the most part, I like rock & roll eccentrics. Ever since the sixties, rock music has been fueled by a potent dose of antiestablishment energy. Janis Joplin, Jim Morrison, and Bob Dylan built a nonconformist stage upon which they gave birth to the eccentricity-as-art movement that Marilyn Manson makes a mint pilfering today.

And don't get me wrong, I like Marilyn Manson. Hell, I liked him way back when he was Alice Cooper. But Marilyn Manson is not a true eccentric because, you just know, the second his concert is over, he neatly drapes his genetically neutered unitard on a hanger for pressing and talks to his broker while he rubs Jergens lotion into the spots where the straps have chafed his heels. Hey, a true eccentric can't turn it off. To own the world's largest collection of buffalo head nickels and then glue every one of them onto your '73 AMC Pacer requires true purity of vision, not to mention the plate in your head.

In the past, people were so much easier to shock. I mean, in the fifties when Milton Berle dressed up on TV in drag, folks watching him would laugh themselves sick. Nowadays, we've become much more open-minded. A television comedian no longer needs to publicly degrade and ridicule his feminine side, but can now lead a fulfilling life as the sardonic host of his very own live Friday night cable show and then go home to a loving family who wholeheartedly supports his other persona—a saucy, miniskirted ingenue named Crissy-Anne. Oh, how I love my Bonnie Bell Strawberry Lip-Smacker!

Seriously, we've all got our eccentricities, and if parading around my bedroom wearing nothing but a bowler hat, an ascot, and a dead fox tied to my fully erect penis while referring to my wife as "the Lady Miller" is wrong, well, I don't want to be right.

Folks, I say we're doing ourselves a great disservice. I think we need the ability to be shocked back in our lives. Not so much, of course, that I'll no longer be allowed to say the word "fuck" more frequently than Joe Pesci when his hand caught in a car door, but enough so that the truly bizarre can once again get their due. Let eccentricity have its day in the sun, and trust me, it'll show up wearing an umbrella hat, carrying a valise full of cat shit, an unstrung tennis racket, and every *Reader's Digest* "Humor in Uniform" ever published stuffed into a Quick Draw McGraw lunch box. And I do mean Quick Draw, and not his evil doppelganger, El Kabong.

Listen, the main reason for the death of eccentricity is that we have identified and therefore demystified many behaviors that were heretofore huddled under the awning of charming idiosyncrasy. Turns out, the reclusive hermit is an agoraphobic; the screaming misanthrope has Tourette's syndrome; and the jovial hayseed who jacks off on his porch all the time . . . uh . . . well, he's just the President of the United States.

Of course, that's just my opinion, I could be wrong.

The End of Accountability

Now, I don't want to get off on a rant here, but when it comes to accountability, this country is in more denial than a sixteen-year-old getting caught by his mother in the bathroom with the swimsuit issue in one hand and himself in the other.

From the child who blames a broken lamp on his imaginary friend Larry Lampbreaker to the adult who sues for wrongful termination because the employee manual didn't say that Xeroxing your bunghole was verboten, to the injured hang glider seeking compensation from the descendants of Sir Isaac Newton, the list of ways we weasel out of accepting blame for stuff is longer than the beep on Leonardo DiCaprio's answering machine.

We've become uncannily adept at not taking responsibility for decisions and actions which may be, to put it kindly, less than wise. Like silicone breast implants. I mean, I understand that it's important to have humongous breasts in case you're ever at the same club as David Lee Roth and you don't want him to ignore you, but how could you actually think that somebody could put sandwich bags full of bathroom grout into your body without side effects?

And whatever happened to corporate accountability? Just once, just once, when I call a company and tell them their product broke down on me, I'd love to hear the drone at the other end of the line say, "Mr. Miller, I'm sorry that happened. It's our fault, and we will immediately ship you out another AssBlaster 2000." Or, you know, whatever the product might be.

And how 'bout the guy who sued Courtney Love a couple of years ago because he got roughed up a little in the mosh pit thing during a concert. Hey, dickwad! You're in the mosh pit at a Hole concert. What the fuck do you think is gonna happen, a decoupage class with Doug Henning?

Our justice system has bigger holes in it than Linda Tripp's fishnets. What's with violent criminals who blame their behavior on the fact that they ate something with sugar in it, and it caused a psychotic episode? Sorry, guys, the coo-coo thing only works for the bird in the Cocoa Puffs commercial, all right? Now strip down and enjoy your cavity search. There's a prize in every box.

We don't do ourselves any favors by being too lenient with criminals. A society thrives on a clear demarcation between right and wrong. What would happen if one day we all decided not to act responsibly and refused to accept the consequences of our actions? I mean, come on . . . We can't all be President.

Bill Clinton is the poster boy for lack of accountability. The only time the buck stops in the Clinton administration is when it's rolled up and jammed into the stripper's G-string.

I'm sure Bill Clinton falls asleep every night absolutely convinced that it was the vast right wing conspiracy dogging him for six long years that drove him into the loving embrace of a young intern. And that's crazy, since we all know that oxygen is the real culprit here, because breathing makes Bill Clinton horny.

This shift into the crybaby mode has to be traced to our generation. In our parents' generation, you sucked it up and walked it off. Nobody gave a rat's ass about being chronically depressed or having low self-esteem or not feeling empowered. You fought the bull and sometimes the bull won and sometimes you won. And it was good and there was wine and people danced and laughed. Sorry, thought I was Hemingway there for a second.

But today, when children turn out poorly, parents blame the schools, other kids, or television. Well, let me offer up another possible reason your kid is a mouth breather, hanging out in a video arcade, bumming tokens to Duke Nukem 3. As a parent, you suck, okay?

And if you suck, the odds are your kid is going to suck. It's not the diet, not the environment, not the media, not the schools. It's you. You suck. And so does your kid.

Come on, folks. This is an easy fix. You've got to do the right thing and take responsibility for your own behavior instead of suing the inventor of the fork because you've got a fat ass. We've all got to toughen up a little. Accountability may not be dead, but it is getting harder to find than a sumo wrestler's belly button.

And it's up to each and every one of us to winnow out the bullshit and call people on it and indeed call ourselves on it when we're at fault. Use that bathroom mirror for something other than braiding your nose hairs. When you're at fault, just look into it and say out loud, "Man, I really, really, really fucked up this time." That's all. It's that simple. Then and only then will we begin to realize that when all is said and done, there's only one person who solely controls your destiny. And that, of course, is Bill Gates.

Of course, that's just my opinion, I could be wrong.

Rock & Roll

Now I don't want to get off on a rant here, but rock & roll will never die. At least that's what I read on the side of the Fuji blimp that was dropping Snapple coupons into the Blockbuster pavilion at the Zima-sponsored Backstreet Boys concert I attended last year. Don't say they're just another New Kids on the Block, 'cause they're not. That's NSync.

Rock & roll started out as the blues, and back then, it was sung by performers with names like "Blind Lemon" Jefferson, "Big Mama" Thornton, and "No Nickname" Williams.

And then there was the pigmentational segue that was Elvis. In the early years, with his jackhammering hips, and that juvenile delinquent sneer, the Boy King embodied the uninhibited, unapologetic sexual freedom of two dogs humping by the side of the road, and damned if all of America didn't slow down and stare at it.

It was only much later, when Elvis went from leaving the building to being the building, that he became the poster boy for pure excess, playing with the three Tarot death cards that every rock star has been dealt: booze, pills, and streaky bacon.

Elvis got me into the tent. When I was a kid, I had a band called the Rants and it taught me about life. Rock & roll was my professor. From John Lennon I learned to question authority, from Robert Plant's androgen-drenched yowl on "Whole Lotta Love" I learned the power of passion, and from Leo Sayer the importance of just kicking back and feeling good about dancing.

As we get closer to a new century, rock & roll is no longer just a driving bass line and four-four time. It's a marketing tool to be packaged and sold to an eager public. And as much as I admire rockers like Neil Young, who have never sold out, not all product endorsements by rockers are bad. Have you tried Ozzy Ozbourne's new alfredo sauce? Dee-licious. "I am ziti man."

As a style of music, rock is in danger of losing its edge. For one thing, it's just not new anymore. It won't be long before the Rolling Stones' tour bus can park in the handicapped spot.

That's why I had to give it to the Sex Pistols. Bunch of drunken, butt-ugly degenerate working-class cockney thugs who never learned how to play their instruments, songs that sounded like a cat being chainsawed inside an airborne Cessna with engine trouble, attitudes that made the Manson Family look like Up with People with a contempt for their audience that almost matched the contempt they had for one another; the instant they started gaining popularity, the nanosecond some pretentious asswipe wrote an article in *Rolling Stone* hailing them as "rock's subversive saviors," what did they do? They broke up. They told us all to go fuck ourselves. Now that is rock & roll.

And the Pistols were smart to get out when they did, 'cause it's inevitable that one generation's hardcore is the next generation's Muzak. Even rap: I guarantee you that one day, your grandkids will be in a dentist's office and they'll hear the Ray Coniff Singers crooning about "Strapping a 'gat to lay the bitch out flat."

The problem may not be that rock & roll sold out but that simply everybody bought into it. MTV did for rock & roll what the full-length mirror did for Liberace. Even our current President ran for office with a Fleetwood Mac tune as his campaign song. True, he never dropped acid, but Bill Clinton's mind is about the only thing that hasn't been blown.

Who are some of my favorites? Well, I kind of like Hole. You watch Courtney Love onstage and that raw aggression is so sexually intimidating, even Clinton's everready manbone would retract like a motorized Volvo antenna.

I was a big fan of Guns N' Roses and I know for a fact that Axl Rose can still belt out the tunes. I hear him every other Wednesday when he's skimming my neighbor's pool.

I read Jewel's new book of poetry last night. It was a real eye-opener. You know what I learned? I found out prejudice is stupid . . . Well, it is!

Beck, totally awesome. Without a doubt *Odelay* is one of the greatest albums people whose opinions I truly respect are pissed off at me for never listening to.

Oasis. You know if the Beatles ever got back together and decided to make a parody of songs by the Wings, this is what they'd sound like.

There was a time when I looked for advice and direction in the lyrics of my favorite rock songs. Looking back on it, it's probably a good thing I couldn't understand a word the lead singer in Molly Hatchet was saying. But I think now rock music is less about deep personal statements and more about simple entertainment.

So to all those people out there who are whining that Metallica sold out when they cut their hair, I say, "Hey, you're thirty-five years old, move out of your parents' house."

As long as there are fourteen-year-old boys, rock & roll will never die. Because what was true in the fifties still holds true today: Playing music will get you laid. I don't know if that's why Beethoven wrote symphonies, but it would sure as hell explain why a deaf guy played the piano.

And there are some other things about rock & roll that will never change also. It will always be the music of rebellion. It will always be frowned on by the establishment and you will never, never understand a single word Bob Dylan is saying.

Of course, that's just my opinion, I could be wrong.

I RANT

The Need for Reason

Now, *Roe* v. *Wade*'s not for everybody, but you do have to concede, at least it was a reasoned decision. And those are becoming rarer than a Nosferatuburger.

Now, I don't want to get off on a rant here, but reason is rapidly becoming harder to find than the plot of *The Thin Red Line*.

On every major social, economic, and political issue of the day, the fringe positions are now as crowded as the exits at a Limp Bizkit concert in Branson, Missouri, while the reasonable middle is as vacant as an interview with Posh Spice.

We are now officially a nation influenced by extremists. You can't sit on the fence anymore without becoming a target for every whack job out there shooting at you from both the right wing and the left wing. Hey, what happened to the rest of the bird?

There just doesn't seem to be a healthy middle ground anymore. Take the death penalty. Believe it or not, I don't always favor lethal injection. Sometimes I think we should use the electric chair and other times the gas chamber or the firing squad. You know, rotate 'em like a good set of tires.

And what about the Clinton impeachment trial, huh? What about the pervasive lack of reason across the entire political spectrum? If Ken Starr had been reasonable, he would've closed up shop when he couldn't nail Clinton on Whitewater. If Clinton were reasonable, he wouldn't keep whipping it out like it was the only lighter in a crack house.

If the Republicans were reasonable, they wouldn't have been so bloodthirsty about finally catching him with his pants down. If the Democrats were reasonable, he would have been shunned like an Amish kid with a nipple ring. And if Hillary was reasonable, she would've long ago said, "My lawyers will be in touch, Captain Hard-On."

And don't even get me started on James Carville. This guy looks like a Muppet that was accidentally washed in hot. You know, I would be much more receptive to Carville if I ever got the sense that he possesses anything even remotely resembling the ability to reason. But there is never any real discussion about anything, it's all just yanking the pull-starter on top of that ugly garlic knot of a head of his and watching him turn into a satanic Chihuahua under a strobe light.

And now with the 2000 election year fast upon us we will be inundated with a conga line of people who have even less of a clue than this current batch of nozzleheads. Pat Buchanan is running, no, make that stumbling, for President. You know who talked Pat Buchanan into running? Me, Leno, Letterman, and Al Gore.

But let's move beyond politics. Because nowhere is there less reason than in our legal system. Everybody's first impulse in this country when something goes wrong is simply to sue. I can't believe that a smoker who admits to smoking all of her life sues the tobacco companies and gets $51 million. Hey, doll, if you're out there watching tonight, turn down the iron lung for a second because I want you to hear this: **WHAT THE FUCK DID YOU THINK WAS GOING TO HAPPEN?** Smoke is a carcinogen. You inhaled it. Case closed. Go rent *How Green Was My Valley*. Just because I get my crank caught in my zipper doesn't mean I can sue Levi Strauss. All right?

You know who else is unreasonable? Moral babysitters. Jerry Falwell, relax. Nobody's trying to turn you gay. Okay? You know why? Because you're a pompous fat-ass. Lighten up, Torquemada, and try some cottage cheese once in a while.

Hey, I'm not suggesting that everybody could be an Einstein if they just let their hair grow out. If everybody was a supergenius, there wouldn't be anybody to make french fries or sell live bait.

I'm just suggesting that we try picking our brains up off the pile of papers they're holding down and see what happens when we plug them in.

There's always going to be people marching to the beat of their own dented drum who reject the concept of logical thought. And those people are always going to wind up ahead of you in line at the DMV. But we can't allow these relatively small extremist factions to take over this country. Because if we cave in and toss aside reason, we're saying yes to a world where a fucking no-talent moron disc jockey named Greaseman can trivialize human torture and then appeal to our sense of decency to let him have his job back, a world where antiabortion zealots wield deadly weapons to demonstrate how precious they hold human life, and a world where a naïve little girl gets two hours of television time to lecture 70 million Americans on the intricacies of subduing your gag reflex . . . ah, fuck it, where's my propeller hat?

Of course, that's just my opinion, I could be wrong.

The Oscars

As originally aired on 3/19/99

Now, I don't want to get off on a rant here, but I'm glad the Oscars are on Sunday this year. That means that no one will see my mortifying guest appearance as Rusty, the web-footed short order cook who's lost his faith, along with the use of his right hand—ironically, the one appendage on his body that was not webbed—in a horrible grill mishap on "Seventh Heaven."

Of course, I'm not in the running for an Oscar this year, because I didn't appear in any movies. Roberto, Tom, Sir Ian, Edward, Nick . . . you're welcome.

Oh, the Oscars, more fun than a barrel of Benignis. I can't wait to watch the preshow and see Joan and Melissa treat best actress nominee Fernanda Montenegro like she's their upstairs maid.

And what are the Academy Awards without Oscar parties. Hey, here's a cool thing to do at an Oscar party.

Whenever the camera cuts to Nicholson in the audience, just scream out, "Fucking Jack . . ." And then take an ice pick six, maybe eight inches long and plunge it straight into your right temple.

Now, it can be difficult to keep in mind that these awards are about the art of filmmaking when so much attention is paid to the glitz and glamour—you know, the limos, the red carpet, the stunning fashions, the bottomless pots of franks and beans . . . I, well, I'm just guessing what it must be like.

Of course, there is a controversy brewing at this year's event. The Lifetime Achievement Award honoring director Elia Kazan. For too long I have remained silent on the controversy surrounding Kazan.

That's because I wanted to wait till he was pushing ninety and make sure he was way too old to be hiring actors. And now that he's on his way out and there's no chance of him ever using me in a film, I'd like to say he's a traitorous, no-good stoolie. Unless, of course, he gets hot again, in which case, he's a timeless visionary.

You know, if there's any justice in the universe, when Kazan accepts his award, he'll have trouble remembering the names of those he wants to thank.

If this year's Oscars had a theme, I would have to say it's history. Three of the best picture nominees were about World War II and the other two were about the Elizabethan era. Quite frankly, I'm amazed that pictures with serious historical content do so well in this country, where people will stand in the freezing rain for four hours to shake hands with Al Roker.

As far as I can tell, *Elizabeth* is about some chick who's kind of nice-looking, then she becomes Queen of England and gets all ugly and bald.

I think *Shakespeare in Love* will win a lot of Oscars this year. It has everything the Academy looks for. Intelligence, costumes, humor, good acting, and nudity. You see, the Academy is mostly comprised of older people who aren't getting laid. They want to go to the movies under the pretense of immersing themselves in the arts while simultaneously hoping they will catch a glimpse of some bare titty.

The Thin Red Line. What can I say? Terry Malick is a genius and so is anyone who understood this film. I believe the plot was last seen wandering shoeless in the Yukon. I really hope Malick wins. Then maybe during his acceptance speech he can tell us what that meandering self-indulgent piece of shit was all about. And I didn't even see it.

Saving Private Ryan. So realistic, I fled to Canada the day it came out. You know, perhaps the greatest thing about *Saving Private Ryan* is the way it's opened up dialogue between the generations. Like, the other day, I asked my eight-and-a-half-year-old son, I said, "Hey, you want to see a gritty, disturbing movie about the sacrifices soldiers made in World War II?" And he said, "No, let's play Nintendo." And I said, "Okay, but this time, I'm Mario, and you're Luigi." And he said, "Okay." So I thank you, Steven Spielberg, as a father and as a man.

Anyway, the envelope please. Here are my predictions:

Tom Hanks will be drunk, abusive, and profane.

Best Director? Well, John Madden did a fantastic job directing *Shakespeare in Love*. But then again anyone who's seen *Elizabeth* knows Mike Ditka was no slouch, either.

Best Actor. Tom Hanks. Foremost actor of our time and the only nominee this year who has done my show.

Best Actress. Tom Hanks. Dressed as a woman in "Bosom Buddies." My show wasn't on yet, so he could not say no.

Supporting Actor. Jimmy Coburn playing an abusive father. Great work, Jimmy. But Ed Harris did my show last season so I am voting for him.

Supporting Actress. Kathy Bates is doing my show next month so I'm picking her unless she cancels, then it's Judi Dench.

And now the nominees for Best Film.

Elizabeth. Period piece about the Queen of England. Great film. Didn't see it. Won't see it. Won't rent it. Will flip by it at the speed of light when it comes on TV.

Life Is Beautiful. A wonderful movie about one man's attempt to divert his son's eyes from the horror of the Holocaust. But it was so tragic, I could not see it.

Saving Private Ryan. Love Hanks, love Spielberg. Too tragic. Did not see it.

Shakespeare in Love. My wife wanted me to see it. So I saw it. She says I loved it.

The Thin Red Line. The tragedies of war in the Pacific Theater. One of my writers said he couldn't follow it. Can't follow it, too tragic. Didn't see it.

Okay, now for my prediction on who will win. Unless the entire academy is gay, it's going to be *Saving Private Ryan.* So my pick is *Elizabeth.*

Of course, that's just my opinion, I could be wrong.

Skepticism

Now, I don't want to get off on a rant here, but everyone's a skeptic these days, and if you don't believe me, well, you just proved my point.

You know from championship boxing matches to peace in Yugoslavia to powertrain warranties written in type smaller than an amoeba's dick on a cold day, Americans now approach everything with lower expectations than a lunchtime john at an "Everything's a Dollar" whorehouse.

Well, the fact is, we have to be skeptical. Think of your mind as a nightclub. Skepticism is the jaded doorman who keeps the riffraff from coming in and asking Bianca Jagger to slow-dance.

So skepticism does serve a purpose. On the other hand, our reflexive disbelief of what we're told by the political, social, and religious establishments leads us into an occasional unholy alliance with what can kindly be described as "foaming at the mouth psychotic lunatics." We like to think of ourselves as street-smart doubting Thomases who can't be fooled by those in power, but the truth is, we'll buy anything if it's packaged with the patchouli-scented whiff of quote "the alternative." Come on, folks, "Deepak Chopra" is Malaysian for Ron Popeil.

And speaking of Popeil . . . You know, you can wrap any bullshit product up in an infomercial with some British guy in a sweater almost as loud as he is and we'll accept it with the breathless, unquestioning faith of a fourteen-year-old girl answering a chain letter. "Hmmm . . . Extracts the moisture out of a heretofore succulent piece of fruit, thereby rendering it better. Sure, I'll take two."

Look, the only way to get people to completely trust you is to speak entirely without any trappings of power. To speak with authority, you must abandon all authority. But that makes you an authority, which means you can't be trusted, which means you have no authority, which means you can be trusted. In other words, when there is no authority, everybody is an authority. You know, if this were 1968, I would be getting so laid with that.

I used to be a skeptic but not anymore, because now I am positive that I am getting screwed. I don't see the glass as half-empty or half-full. As a matter of fact, I don't even see the glass because the fucking kid at Pottery Barn who promised me the champagne flutes would be here in time for my Oscar party no doubt never even put the order in and I'm serving my guests Moët & Chandon in Welch's grape jelly jars commemorating the birth of Bamm Bamm Rubble.

And skepticism is everywhere. I took my nine-year-old to see the cartoon *Anastasia*. Afterward, I said, "What did you think?" He said, "She's definitely had a boob job."

Oh, it all starts to wear on you and when I need to refresh my gray tired soul from the ravages of skepticism, I look no further than the kindly face of Dr. Jack Kevorkian. Such faith. Such honesty. Doesn't lie, doesn't waver, just firmly believes in the healing power of death. God love ya, Jackie. Keep on snuffin'.

Skeptics had a field day with the Lewis–Holyfield fight last year. But even with something that obvious, you'll still get your cockeyed optimistic innocent who argues that the judge from New Jersey really scored the fight the way she saw it. Please. This woman had car keys snagged on her little toe from when Don King pulled her out of his pocket. She couldn't have been more bought if she had a bar code stamped on her forehead.

And Don King comes off like Hank Fonda in *The Grapes of Wrath* when you stack him up next to the prevaricator in chief, William Jefferson Clinton—if that is indeed your name, sir.

Like Michael Jordan with basketball and Mark McGwire with home runs, Bill Clinton has taken lying and elevated it to an exalted art form, setting new levels in fibbery that future generations can only hope to aspire to. Watching

Clinton lie is like watching Secretariat in the stretch at the Belmont Stakes. It's really quite stirring. You realize you are witnessing a beautiful creature who's been bred and trained to perform one task instinctively, without thought or reservation, like a finely tuned machine. Only difference being, Clinton was put out to stud before retirement.

Of course, that's just my opinion, I could be wrong.

Bad Taste

ow, I don't want to get off on a rant here, but is there anything that goes down smoother than somebody else's bad taste? My definition of bad taste? Owning anything with the *Mona Lisa* on it that isn't the actual *Mona Lisa*.

The lowbrow aesthetic is as prevalent in our culture as fringed T-shirts saying I'M DUCKING FISGUSTED.

Bad taste is the uncanny ability to take any experience, no matter how pure and beautiful, and distill it down to its most cringe-worthy elements. It's the belief that the greatest tribute one can pay to the infinite joys of parenthood is a limited edition porcelain figurine of a curly-haired tot with saucer eyes and a massive Vanna White–sized head, sitting on a potty below a little plaque that reads MY FIRST WEEWEE.

Bad taste is having the subtlety and depth of feeling to realize that if the *Venus de Milo* was a great work of art and

Marilyn Monroe was a great movie star, then a *Venus de Milo* with Marilyn Monroe's head is even greater yet, and if that *Venus de Marilyn* happens to be outfitted with a water spout at the mouth and hot and cold taps where the breasts are, then even an everyday shower can be a monument to true beauty.

Accuse me of stereotyping, but when I see people with bad taste, I believe I know their lives through their uniquely tacky thumbprint. I saw a guy the other day who was perfect. He had on navy blue polyester Hagar slacks with brown snakeskin cowboy boots and a pink muscle shirt with green stripes. This guy had sideburns like I haven't seen since TBS last ran *Play Misty for Me,* topped with a comb-over that looked like it had been done by a spider on Xanax. Now, I know this man. He does not drive a Saab. He will only refer to pasta as "noodles." There are jumper cables sitting on his dining room table. His name is Don, but he goes by Ricky, which confuses relatives who want to buy him bowling shirts.

His wife's name is June, but he calls her Candy, except when she dips below four hundred pounds, he then calls her Dot. When he wants to make love, he winks at her and says, "Doggy needs a walk," which prompts her to put on a miniskirt, which is comprised of more black velvet than the den of a West Virginia lottery winner. Then he puts on the Oak Ridge Boys to camouflage the squeak of Dot's gigantic ass on his sky blue Naugahyde recliner, which they have to use because he hurt his back throwing a half a keg of beer through the windshield of his ex-wife's boyfriend's Dodge Charger. Ricky times his thrusts with the "woo-boppa, woo-boppa, woo-boppa mao mao" part of the song "Elvira" and attempts to hold off his orgasm by trying to remember the nicknames of Richard Petty's pit crew . . . but then he remembers the fuel man Nick was named "Boob," causing him to blow his wad. So Don slash Ricky pinches the filter off one of Candy slash Dot's Virginia Slims and grabs the remote to try to find a fishing show or a lumberjack competition and . . . and . . . I'm lost, what was this rant about? Oh yeah, these people have really bad taste.

And never forget, bad taste is simply that. Scholars may hail this cultural flotsam and jetsam as American "folk art," but they're missing the point. The point is, **IT'S CRAP.** And that's why we love it. It's purely representational, purely visceral, nothing to understand, nothing to ponder. The beer cans go in the hat, the tubes go in the beer, the beer goes in your mouth. Poetic in its simplicity.

But even though there's a part of each of us that clings to bad taste like a Garfield suction cup doll on the inside windshield of an AMC Pacer, there are certain rules of decorum that must never be violated.

Cheese should never come in a spray can. Unless, of course, you're trying to market a new deodorant for the French.

And never order anything from the Franklin Mint. You know why they call it a mint? Because right after their uberjunk arrives in the mail, that is exactly what you need to take the shitty taste out of your mouth.

And oh yeah, if any of you out there are wearing a lucky horseshoe belt buckle, I want you to stop, take a beat, and think about your life. That's it. Put your pricing gun back in your pricing gun holster for a minute and actually think about your life. Now, how lucky has that belt buckle really been for you? You see my point, Jimmy Jimmy Jo-Jo?

Finally, some people will say bad taste is purely subjective, because it's a matter of personal likes and dislikes. Well, I disagree. I think it's inherently objective, because it's a matter of my personal likes and dislikes. You see, if you think your two-tone, lime green, fur-lined six-inch platform shoes are in good taste, well then, you're wrong. And you know who made me the arbiter of taste? Well, you did, Dr. Nehru, when you walked in with two dead fucking Muppets on your feet.

Of course, that's just my opinion, I could be wrong.

U.S. as Global Police

As originally aired on 4/9/99

Now, I don't want to get off on a rant here, but much like the crew of the starship *Enterprise* visiting a new planet, the United States always starts out by stating we have no intention of interfering with a nation's infrastructure, but the next thing you know, we're walking around Kosovo like Barney Fife in lederhosen.

Now, there are many laudable reasons for the United States to serve as a global policeman. For one thing, it pisses off the French. But it's also very risky. Serbian leaders may characterize the current situation in Yugoslavia as nothing more than a domestic squabble, but any cop will tell you that's the most dangerous kind of call to answer.

This war in Kosovo must be serious, because this is the first crisis that hasn't just been President Clinton's attempt to rodeo-clown our attention away from some seedy indiscretion.

I just hope that when all this global busywork is finished and the Kosovars are back in their homes, they don't forget the help we gave them and jack up our oil prices. Wait a minute, Kosovo doesn't have vast oil supplies. Hey, what the hell are we even doing there?

I'll be honest with you, most of the time I'd rather not get involved in other people's blood feuds. Some of these grudges run deeper than the crack of Ernest Borgnine's ass. I'm sorry, Tova. Apparently, the Serbian people's desire to rid Kosovo of the ethnic Albanians stems from a defeat they suffered over six centuries ago at the hands of the Ottoman Turks. The Ottomans, if memory serves, were able to secure victory by hiding soldiers inside a huge cushioned footstool they built and offering it to the Serbs as a gift. Or wait, was that the Hassocks?

Got a little civil insurrection under way right here. Anyway, justifying police actions since the fall of the Soviet Union has been a real problem for America because we can no longer rely on the one-size-fits-all political excuse, "We were fighting communism." Boy, the Commies . . . What a great enemy, huh? A combination of Professor Moriarty, Ming the Merciless, and Craig Kilborn all rolled up into one. Now, Lenin's tomb is a recycling bin for old Stoli bottles, and Yeltsin's more hammered than Bob Vila's left thumb.

But in selecting our enemies, there's always been one constant: America hates bullies. Make no mistake. This country is the greatest country in the world, because we've got a national conscience and at least some of the time, in between Oval Office blowjobs, we act on it.

When some jackass finally yanks our chain long enough and we drop two hundred tons of explosives on him, the wussier countries of the world like to accuse us of being cowboys. Okay, Señor Speedo, you win. That's right. We're Gary goddamn Cooper, and you know what? Saddle up and get in the posse or shut the fuck up. All right?

And don't expect us to be embarrassed about our wading into Kosovo. You know why? We've already got Grenada on our résumé. Okay? We entered into Grenada simply because some Castro-backed steel drum band was building the Ricky Ricardo Memorial Airstrip there.

So after connecting through Atlanta, our boys stormed the beaches, and before you could say "I got my medical degree from the University of Gilligan," the fighting was over. You know, to this day, the people of Grenada have no idea what happened. They just talk about that one weird weekend when all the tourists were so pissed off and rude.

I'll tell you one thing about Grenada, at least we had to get up off the couch, put on something green, and actually go there. Watching the battle for Kosovo on CNN, I'm struck by how similar it is to a Nintendo game. As a matter of fact, you probably have kids at home who could fly a Stealth bomber if their feet could only reach the pedals. And when I say a "Nintendo war," I don't just mean the fact that we can push a button in a submarine and launch a missile that flies eight hundred miles before exploding its target. I'm also talking about the fact that our enemies are brightly colored cartoon creatures whom we defeat by jumping on their heads at exactly the right moment. Wait, that actually is Nintendo. What channel is CNN on?

Look, I'm never happy to see America at war. But admit it. It feels great to hate again with reckless abandon. Doesn't it? Huh? Slobodan Milosevic is a monster. Even by the way his first name trips off your tongue—Slobodan—you can just tell, he's begging for an ass kicking.

Now, I'm not sure that the air war is the total answer, but then again, I would have never let Luke Perry return to "90210." And I worry about sending in ground troops. But tell me something. When did we take assassination off the menu? Huh? I read that, so far, this little Balkan junket has cost us $500 million. Why not take one one-hundredth of that, $5 million American, and pay Stosh the bodyguard to leave Sloby's back door open one night. Then send some jacked-up ex-CIA cyberninja over there with one of those tape on the handle/Michael Corleone pistols and tell him to make sure that the last words Milosevic ever hears are "Consider yourself cleansed, motherfucker."

Of course, that's just my opinion, I could be wrong.

Charity &
Philanthropy

As originally aired on 4/9/99

Now, I don't want to get off on a rant here, but from slimy televangelists to Greenpeace enviro-geeks to the interminable PBS pledge break that cuts in just as the cheetah is about to whack the gazelle, Americans are increasingly swamped with requests to give their hard-earned money away to charity. You can't get through the day any more without seeing more outstretched hands than a Bob Fosse finale.

Now, look, obviously, I'm all for charity, except when aging hippies use it as a name for their daughter. This is the land of plenty and most of us are damn fortunate that we were hooked up to the embryo static line when the drop zone was over North America. Just your blind luck for being in the right place at the right time should make you *want* to do right by the disenfranchised among us.

And really, how much money does one person need? You know, I'm not sure, but I will tell you when I'm closing in on it.

Now, let's be honest with each other. A lot of people give to charity for one reason and one reason alone. They fear the wrath of the Almighty. They don't care about the whales, never watch a telethon, couldn't give a rat's ass about poverty. Cut the checks for one reason. Sucking up to God.

But if drawing the ire of the Supreme Being isn't really a bee in your bonnet, there's an extra incentive to be generous: You can deduct charitable donations from your income taxes. So you tell me. Why is it that if I give a buck to that sunburned guy and his dog at the end of the off-ramp and I demand a receipt for two bucks, all of a sudden I'm a bad guy.

Truth be told, on the giving scale, I'm about average: When an organization sends me personalized address labels along with a request for a donation, I use the labels without sending them anything, but at least I feel guilty about it . . . about three or four labels into the packet.

I also give $100 a month to a kid in Africa. People say that's great, but actually I was over there in the Peace Corps and I think he might really be mine.

Of course I'm kidding. For me, charity is keeping six bald losers whom their union insists on calling "writers" employed in spite of their drunken binges and $900-a-month phone sex bills without firing their unfunny fat asses for making me try to sell their hackneyed "it should be me out there" lines of witless dung.

You know, generosity shows itself in many guises. Donating money is one way to help. But you can also donate time and energy. Take me, for example. I'm currently working with my best friend in his basement lab every weekend trying to figure out a way to give cancer to cancer. It's crazy, but I think it just might work.

Look, give a man a fish, he eats for a day; teach a man to fish and he eats for a lifetime. But teach a man to be a fish, and he can eat himself. Teach a man to eat himself, and fish no longer matter.

So that's my Good Samaritan profile and you know something? It works for me. And I think most Americans have their priorities straight when it comes to helping their fellow man. But when the philanthropic turns bureaucratic, well, that's when things start to get really really ugly.

Charity has become big business. And charitable organizations use a range of guilt-inducing techniques to play exquisitely on our sense of obligation like Lurch on a harpsichord.

Why can't I satisfy my sweet tooth without it now being some sort of a political statement? Like Ben and Jerry telling me that a portion of the proceeds from their ice cream is now going to save the endangered albino mudskippers of the Galápagos. Hey, maybe I just want the fucking ice cream. All right? Maybe I got a bug up my ass about albino mudskippers. And hey, how much cheaper would the ice cream be if you weren't giving some of the profits away? How's about you lower the price and let me decide what jag-off species I want to prop up, okay? Listen, boys, you caught a cosmic break in the frozen dessert field. Don't get all gorillas in the misty-eyed on me. Just comb your beards, churn the butterfat, and get me my Monkey Chunky Hunky Bunky, all right?

But you know what my biggest beef about present-day charity is? I thought it was supposed to begin at home. And I don't happen to live in Kosovo. We level the place, then we offer to pay to rebuild it. Now, maybe it's the right thing to do, but I just want to be sure that we're going Dutch with the Netherlands on this, okay? 'Cause if I'm a street person walking around Boston in a pair of Kleenex boxes for shoes and a dropcloth muumuu and I look into the window of a *USA Today* dispenser and see this nonsense staring out at me from the front page, I'm going to feel pretty justified about constantly screaming "Bullshit! Bullshit! Bullshit!" at the top of my lungs for the last seventeen years.

Of course, that's just my opinion, I could be wrong.

College Life

ow, I don't want to get off on a rant here, but is there any four- to ten-year period of your life more glorious than college?

Ah, college. What other institution charges you ninety grand to prepare you for a $20,000-a-year job?

And by the way, I don't think you should have to pay back college loans unless you get a job in your field. Put some pressure on the school. If I can't pay my bills, I'm not paying yours.

When I went to college, I lived on campus, and the guys I hung out with made the characters in *Revenge of the Nerds* look like the Rat Pack in 1962. I myself made that kid Booger look like Remington Steele. I remember finally breaking down and trying to wash a pair of socks by shaking them around in a rinsed-out Skippy peanut butter jar full of hot water and a squeeze of Colgate Tartar Control tooth-paste.

Now, my sophomore year, I had three completely differ-ent roommates: Sidney was a grade-grubber, Tom was a ladies' man, and then there was Carver. Carver was a total stoner. He smoked more bud on an average day than Ziggy Marley's entire band the night before they had to go through customs. Carver showed me that the real fun to be derived from a Frisbee was not in throwing it or catching it, but in staring at it for hours on end and marveling at "how fuckin' round it is, man!"

The one thing I did learn right off the bat is, never have a roommate who's really good-looking unless you like sleeping out in the hall using a bag of Cheetos for a pillow. Fortunately, my junior year roommate Wayne and I got along really well. We each had a signal to use to let the other know we were in bed with a girl, so don't come in. His sign was, he'd leave a belt hanging on the doorknob. My sign was, Hell would freeze over. So it worked out well for both of us.

Co-ed dorms are God's little joke on postadolescent males. At no time in your life will you ever again be so horny, and living so close to so many women who will have absolutely nothing to do with you.

Nowadays, certain universities make you get written permission from somebody before you can have any physi-cal contact with them. Oh that's just great, you're pasty-faced, lonely, horny, insecure . . . and now, in addition to breaking the news to your date that you're going to have to go dutch with her at the Souplantation 'cause you blew all your money on a keggerator, she's also gotta write a three-page essay on why she'd like to accompany you back to the pathetic little Yasmine Bleeth–poster-decorated corner of hell that you call a dorm room and that you share with a guy named "Spoogie" whose rigorous masturbation schedule means that he only leaves the room for meals and to man his shift in the line for *Phantom Menace* tickets—but Spoogie's out tonight at the clinic, getting that thing looked at, and you're just praying your date won't laugh at you when you read her the liner notes from *Melon Collie and the Infinite Sadness* in a pathetic attempt to get her in the mood to submit to your clumsy, feeble gropings, and your way-too-sloppy ear kisses, oh, you suave bastard, you.

Well, you're not there to fornicate anyway, you're there to get a sheepskin, not a lambskin. And I'm beginning to think it doesn't really matter where you get it from. There's no difference between Ivy League schools and other colleges. Some of my best friends are from Ivy League schools and their hobbies are watchin' "CatDog" and lighting each other's farts.

And what is this obsession with degrees, anyway? Liberal arts? That's not a degree, that's a wall hanging. Philosophy majors? The last guy to get a job out of his philosophy degree was your philosophy professor.

Bottom line, kids: College is a way station, the last convenience store before the desert of responsibility. It's a place to separate the people who want to study and move on to a fulfilling lifelong career from the geniuses who want to drop maraschino cherries out of their ass into a shot glass for the glory of drinking a free tequila shot out of the same glass.

And not that there's anything wrong with kids who decide that college isn't for them. Look at Bill Gates. He dropped out of Harvard and then went on to become the richest man in the universe. But can you imagine how much richer he would be right now if he just had his degree?

Of course, that's just my opinion, I could be wrong.

Doctors

Now, I don't want to get off on a rant here, but the medical profession is in big trouble—and not only because George Clooney has left.

Gone are the days when you could visit your GP and receive treatment for a wide variety of maladies. Medicine today is highly highly specialized. Even for something as simple and straightforward as penile lengthening, you've got to see separate doctors for the head and the shaft now. So I've heard.

Now, I like doctors. But to me, there's one man who embodies all the best qualities a physician should have. Expertise, a caring nature, and an undying passion to put the patient's needs above all else. Dr. Leonard "Bones" McCoy. For five years, Bones cared for the starship *Enterprise* and its entire crew. Remember when Kirk got that alien clap? Huh? Bones took care of it. And when Sulu and

Chekhov exchanged genitalia in a transporter malfunction? Bones took care of it. Or that time Spock couldn't get back to Vulcan for his once-every-seven-year fuck and he did that Tribble? Bones took care of the Tribble quietly and discretely. Bones, if you're somewhere out there tonight, you are a doctor, damn it. And a damn fine one at that.

Now, when selecting a doctor, there are simple things you can do to help ensure finding a conscientious, quality professional. For example, the magazines in a doctor's office can tell you how prompt he is in keeping appointments.

If the teeth of every celebrity pictured in them have been blacked out with a ballpoint pen, patients are waiting longer than they should. I know people were waiting for me to say "Godot" at the DMV. But Godot wasn't waiting and if I had said "Vladimir" and "Estragon," I'd have been waiting even longer for a laugh.

One thing even doctors will tell you is that they can make mistakes. Just don't tell it to me as you are anesthetizing me for surgery. I had to go in for a minor procedure once and just as I was going under, I could've sworn I heard calypso music and saw my doctor dancing around wearing a pair of coconut tits. But later, they said it was just the gas. And then daylight came, and I went home.

But the real problems for doctors nowadays are the HMOs. And if doctors have a hard time with the HMOs, it's even tougher on patients, who have to navigate through a sprawling, impersonal ganglion of voice-directed, automated phone instructions and reams of paperwork, all for the privilege of sitting for hours in a waiting room with magazines that are so dated, there's one called *Modern Leeching Monthly*, then being herded into an examining room that has all the warmth and charm of an Orwellian interrogation chamber, where you have to wait another hour or two but this time while wearing a gown made out of a Handi Wipe and a Wonder Bread twist tie that does about as much to cover you up as a paper ruffle on a lamb chop. Then the doctor, a twitchy drone with a nebulous accent who graduated from the Bar Code Academy of Medicine in the Canary Islands, starts doing things to you that would be considered rude inside Devil's Island. And to add insult to injury, when it's all over, they won't even validate your fucking parking.

And if you don't have insurance, don't even think about trying to get a doctor to look at you. When you're not insured, doctors act like you've got some kind of a disease or something.

Many of us are intimidated by doctors. Well, let me see if I can demystify them for you. A doctor is an ordinary human being just like you or me, except they're smarter, better, and possess godlike powers over life and death.

And I really do like doctors. I happen to believe they deserve to make a lot of money, and it always surprises me how many people get bent out of shape about their fees. For example, every couple years, I have to see a proctologist for a colonoscopy. Now, a colonoscopy, for the uninitiated, is that long dolly shot Scorsese did in *GoodFellas* with your pooper being the Copacabana. Now, my proctologist is a man who saw me a few times and, shall we say, rectified a relatively minor problem. So what if after I paid him he actually went out and bought a top-of-the-line forty-foot racing sloop and named it *Dennis Miller's Ass?* The point is, I'm better.

But no matter what your opinion may be of doctors, you'd better get used to dealing with them because as the warranty on your body starts to run out, you'll be spending more time in the shop than an E-Type Jag.

Hey, whether they're called shamans, medicine men, or high priests, all cultures celebrate their healers. And I respect doctors for the awesome responsibility they take on by swearing a sacred oath to protect my health. And you know something? I don't care about bedside manner or whether there's proper feng shui in the reception area. Just do your job and do it well and you will earn my hopefully undying gratitude. That being said, don't ever, ever try any of that Patch Adams shit on me. Okay? I don't care how sick I am, you come after me with a clown nose and a squirting stethoscope, and I will kick you in the nuts so hard, you won't be needin' helium to make your voice go that high.

Of course, that's just my opinion, I could be wrong.

Popularity & Charisma

Now, I don't want to get off on a rant here, but why do some people have so much popularity and charisma they can coast through life on a pretty smile and good hair, while the rest of us stumble around the track like Boris Yeltsin running the Kentucky Derby in a horse suit?

When you're young, all you care about is having lots of friends. Then, as you mature, you realize there are more important things, like having lots of friends who are less successful than you are.

Popularity is that rare nexus that's created when beauty, charm, and that certain *je ne sais quoi* converge with public approval and large heaving breasts.

What makes certain people popular? That depends. In third grade, it's the simple ability to stuff up your nose with two dimes. In the grown-up world, it boils down to one of three things: money, good looks, or power. And if you're blessed enough to have all three, well, all I can say is, fuck you.

Being popular means being liked, and there's a certain responsibility that goes along with being liked, because you are now in a position to let people down. See, if people think you're an asshole, you can't disappoint them. And that's how much I love people. To prevent them from being disappointed in me, I act like an asshole. Now, I know what you're thinking. Are people disappointed if I'm not as big an asshole as they expect? All I can say is, so far, it has not been a problem.

Now, I'm not saying I don't have any friends. Far from it. But the friends I do have don't have any friends. Big difference.

Look, I admit, nowadays, I have a certain amount of TV-induced popularity, but I'm conflicted about it. I like to be the outsider, the rabble-rouser, the iconoclast, but I also like a nice seat at the Laker game. On the one hand, I don't care what other people think of me; but on the other hand, I want to be remembered as the guy who didn't care what other people thought of him.

Now, here's where popularity and charisma diverge: You can buy popularity, but if you aren't born with charisma, you'll never have it. Charisma is what makes one man a skinny grandfather with bad teeth repeating the same story over and over since 1964 and another man Mick Jagger singing "Satisfaction" to a stadium full of screaming fans at three hundred bucks a head.

Charisma is also what allows people to tell you something that isn't true and make you believe it's fact. It's the people who run the pyramid schemes, the people who tell you one thing and then do another. It's the people who lie right to your face and make you love them for it. In a nutsack, it's William Jefferson Clinton. Clinton's got that rare sort of charisma that makes women want to bang him even as he's apologizing for being a two-timer.

Completely understanding someone's charisma has always been difficult for me. Brad Pitt, for example. Yeah, there's the shine in the eyes, the effervescent smile, the silken blond hair and nicely understated acting style. Yeah, yeah, yeah. I get all that. But where's the charisma?

I've actually heard people say Bill Gates has charisma. For the life of me, why do people go nuts over this guy? Glasses that would be too big for the Teddy Roosevelt face on Mount Rushmore. Hair that looks like it's been styled by a drunken one-armed gnome trying to balance himself on a stepladder, and suits from the Don Knotts "Three's Company" line. What is it that makes Gates so goddamned charismatic? Oh yeah. Eighty tetratrillion dollars. Sorry.

Hey, maybe it's good that true charisma occurs so rarely, because when it does, it's so often misused. Stalin, Jim Jones, Susan Powter . . . As for me, if I did have that indefinable quality that makes all mankind want to do your bidding, I wouldn't try to stir the masses to violence or hatred.

In fact, as I faced a stadium full of enraptured followers chanting my name in an ecstasy of worship, my message would be simple and direct: "You two in the front row, go mow my lawn. The rest of you, get the fuck out of here. You're really creeping me out."

Of course, that's just my opinion, I could be wrong.

Pets

According to a new study, more and more veterinarians are now prescribing Prozac for dogs. You know, unless Prozac can grow back a new set of balls, I'm pretty sure Scruffles isn't gonna be snapping out of his funk. Okay?

Prozac for dogs, huh? Well, why not? With all the lines in our wishy-washy culture being blurred on a daily basis, why not convert man's best friend into man's best codependent partner?

Now, I don't want to get off on a rant here, but lately it's become unfashionable to call your animal a "pet," because it implies ownership and unequal status. The politically correct term is "animal companion." Oh, shut up! I'm sick of this stupid word-parsing crap. It's a pet, all right? It's not an equal relationship, and we both like it better that way. Fido will be my animal companion the day he follows **ME** around with a Baggie picking up my shit. All right?

Dogs know their place and they have for eons. And don't forget, one of our eons is worth seven of theirs. Scientists believe that dogs were the first animals to share living quarters with humans, about forty thousand years ago. Cats and in-laws came along much much later. Different dogs are bred for different tasks. Hunting, herding, protection, fast-food pitchmen. Oh, that little Chihuahua is in for a big big comedown when they don't pick up his option. I mean, what else is he going to do? Unless of course, Calista Flockhart decides to race in the Iditarod.

Domestic animals are continuing to evolve to meet man's needs and this process is being helped along dramatically by advances made in biogenetic engineering. Experts in this field say that in the future, the average family pet will provide the comradeship, the companionship, and the protection of a dog while retaining the less dependent, less needy personality of a cat.

Shortly thereafter, this unique animal of the future will possess udders that deliver high-quality prepasteurized 2 percent milk and hindquarters that yield a weekly supply of a lean, beeflike meat which can be easily sliced off with minimum discomfort to your trusty friend. Now, once again, these goals are years away from being achieved, but you don't want to rush biogenetic engineering, something weird could happen.

But amid all this pet manipulation, there are many well-intentioned but mistaken notions about pets. One common error people make with pets is overgrooming. Your poodle shouldn't look like a topiary plant, okay? And your dog doesn't need a wardrobe that would make Joan Collins jealous. Trust me: No dog wants to wear a cowboy hat and chaps unless it's looking to bang Rin Tin Tin.

And don't overfeed your animal. My friend had a dog named Chickie that he used to feed ice cream to every day until it looked like a furry watermelon. He would yell, "Want some 'scream, Chickie?" and the dog would waddle over for his daily ration. And Chickie finally keeled over after eating a big hunk of kielbasa and never had 'scream again. How do you go on? I don't know. I believe Edmund Hillary said you put one foot in front of the other.

Now, I myself am a pet person. Always have been, always will be. When I was a kid, my mother bought me a turtle. I named him Petey. Now, Petey was shy and for the first couple of days, I noticed that Petey just stayed in his shell. Then I noticed Petey didn't like any of the lettuce I fed him and he really couldn't swim. And finally it dawned on me . . . Petey was a rock. But I didn't care. Because he was my Petey.

You know, nowadays, my dog Kilborn is constantly scooting his ass across the carpet. And you know something? I'm kicking myself now, because I should have never let him watch me do that in the first place.

But for the most part, I rule my pets with an iron chew toy. I'll be damned if I'm going to be pussy-whipped by some cat. Cats have a will of their own. That's why you never hear of a seeing-eye cat. Totally useless unless the blind guy does a lot of sleeping followed by a frisky scamper along a book-shelf.

I find myself a little more sympathetic toward dogs than cats. I once even took my dog to a pet psychotherapist to find out why it would not stop humping my leg. I'm glad I did, because it turned out that the problem wasn't with him, it was with me. Evidently, I was, you know, putting out signals I was not aware of.

Listen, I love pets, you love pets, we all love pets. Just don't let things get out of hand to the point where your pets overrun your life or your household. You ever visit the home of a multiple cat owner? Well, first of all, there's the smell, which I can't begin to describe except to say, imagine if Glade made an air freshener in a fragrance called Ass.

You know, I don't care how clean or diligent you are, once you've got more cats than the Jerusalem phone book living under your roof, your house is permanently enveloped in the kind of toxic stench that makes the reek of a Bombay slaughterhouse smell like freshly baked Toll House cookies.

Bottom line, if you've got over twenty cats in your house, remember each one of them has nine lives and you have none, so if they're really your friends, then maybe they'll let you borrow one.

Of course, that's just my opinion, I could be wrong.

Buying a House

ow, I don't want to get off on a rant here, but buying a home is a process much like bringing a baby into this world. It's a huge undertaking that frays your nerves, saps your energy, tries your patience, and oh yeah, the woman does most of the work.

Whether you're giving a down payment of dried elk meat to a fast-talking igloo salesman from Century 21 Below or building a Xanadu for your no-talent mistress, buying a home is a primal part of the human experience, transcending culture and class while uniting all of humankind in the time-honored ritual of getting screwed out of lots and lots of money.

When I bought my first home, I was surprised by how many people were involved: There was my agent, the seller's agent, the mortgage broker, the inspector, and strangely enough, three members of the rock band Journey. I never figured out what they were doing there, but Steve Perry saved me three grand by spotting a leak in the water heater. I tried to pay him, but he said, no, that's what the band does nowadays: They travel the country, help out folks in need, and then move on. He said that's where their "journey" had taken them.

For me personally, one of the most rewarding parts of having my own show has been helping people who work for me own their own homes.

All of my employees live behind my estate in a small enclave called MillerTown, which is comprised of row after row of squalid dirt-floored shacks the payments for which are deducted from their checks, and whatever is left over is given to them in the form of Dennis-dollars which they can then spend at the MillerTown Market.

Hey, there is no greater joy than the simple realization that you own a home. But getting to that point invariably involves careful navigation through the narrow straits of the free enterprise system. As an aid to you, the potential home buyer, I'm going to play codebreaker here and decipher some of the real estate ad terminology you will encounter on your journey home.

"Charming" means small. "Cute" means small. "Quaint" means old and small. "Airy, spacious, and big" means small.

"Conveniently located" means it's built beneath a freeway overpass.

"Needs tender loving care." Yeah, like Ralph Fiennes in *The English Patient*.

"Ocean view." Uh-huh. On a stepladder, in the attic, with a telescope.

And finally, "Well lit." "Well lit" means a million-watt searchlight from the prison for the criminally insane across the street shines directly into your bedroom every night.

Now, you also have to get your finances in order before you can go house hunting. Remember when you thought taxes were for squares and you were too cool to pay them? You might want to clear that up, Shaggy, before you go for the mortgage app. on that haunted house, okay?

And keep in mind, you never want to work with a mortgage broker who says, "Man, I wish I could buy a house someday." Now, even though interest rates are currently favorable, it is still not easy. The paperwork is harder to understand than Jar Jar Binks on Novocain.

I remember applying for my first mortgage and I got passed around like a goatskin flask at a Dead concert.

But eventually, you machete your way through the thick bureaucratic undergrowth of paperwork, and the mortgage bwana shepherds you into the lost kingdom of Escrow. Now, escrow involves working with a group of people roughly the size of Darryl Strawberry's legal team.

All you have to do is go into their office and sign more forms than there are liability waivers for a White House internship. If all goes well, after a few weeks, you'll close escrow. The closing is a traditional procedure, where, before you can officially call a house your own, you must first lie facedown over a desk while everyone involved with the purchase of your new home . . . the seller, the real estate agent, the lender, the escrow officer, the insurance agent, the mortgage broker, everybody's assistants, and the Sparklet's guy who just happens to be in the office at that time . . . all take turns fucking you in the ass.

Of course, that's just my opinion, I could be wrong.

Models

ou know, when it comes to the subject of modeling, I know what I'm talking about. I don't mention it much, but before I got into comedy, I was an ass model for medical journals. Not proud of it. Not ashamed of it, either.

Now, I don't want to get off on a rant here, but when you see models gathered at a New York City nightspot surrounded by a fawning entourage, it looks very, very glamorous. And you know why? Because it is fucking glamorous, all right. And that's what drives us crazy. It's not that they're beautiful people who *look* like they're having more fun than you. They *are* beautiful people *having* more fun than you. Let's face facts, there are people in Kosovo having more fun than you.

There's no arguing that models get preferential treatment just because they're models. But at least it's honest. I mean, let's quit bullshitting each other. Looks make the world go round. The prettier you are, the better your life. Makeup case closed. And, you know, if you have the right look, it all happens really quickly. One day you're the coltish beauty mixing the corn dog batter at Hot Dog on a Stick, and the next day you're on a hotel balcony in Paris at sunrise and Bono is asking you how you like your eggs.

But it's not all glamour. Modeling is cutthroat at every level. Even baby modeling. Just when you're getting the hang of sitting in a Michelin tire, along comes a cuddlier kid with bigger eyes and more dimples, and next thing you know, you're the fussy brat with the loaded diaper in the background of the Huggies ad.

There are all types of models. There are hand models who advertise gloves, rings, and dishwashing liquid. There are leg models who help sell stockings, shoes, and razors. And then there are breast models who help sell bras, blouses, and swimsuits . . . and beer, tires, lawn mowers, socks, golf clubs, pest-control services, shock absorbers, cheese, paneling, toothpaste.

Then there's the average-looking models: the chunky dad on the John Deere tractor; the gingham-aproned, has-all-the-answers mom; and my personal favorite, the guy who *needs* Mylanta. That combination of droopy eyes and tight grimace. You know, it must be hell to go through life knowing you were born with a face that conveys the message: "I have painful gas."

You know, even if you are stunning, it takes more than good looks to be a model. It takes guts. You face constant rejection, enormous pressure, and lots of middle-aged guys with ponytails driving around in Paco Rabanne–drenched Corvettes who call themselves "producers" and complain that there's no topless shots in your portfolio.

Young models are chum for asshole sharks. How ironic that the most exquisite-looking people in the world should end up choosing the profession that requires them to spend all day by the phone waiting for the most hideous people to call them.

There are some guys who only date models. Donald Trump has a different model on his doughy arm every night. Yeah, well, believe me, it's not his choice, one night with Trump is like a winter night in Norway. It seems like six months.

Guys like Trump date lots of models, but the tiny peter principle kicks in when it comes to dating supermodels. Now, what is the difference between a model and a super-model? Well, a regular model will look at you and tell you to fuck off, but a supermodel doesn't even have to look at you to tell you to go fuck off.

The era of the supermodel began when Linda Evangelista uttered the now infamous remark: "I don't get out of bed for less than $10,000 a day." I hope you've all noticed, Linda hasn't been out of bed for about thirteen months now.

Don't waste your energy being jealous of models. Sure, they're the best of show of the human race, but let's not forget that their careers can be shorter than Mini-Me bending over to pick up Dr. Evil's monocle.

And that's the hardest part of a model's career: knowing when to bow out gracefully. There's no Senior Tour here, folks. Only a handful get the lucrative makeup deals or acting jobs. The ones who don't are left to audition for housecoat ads in *Parade* magazine or get so much plastic surgery that their face is eventually tied back like the end of a roll of braunschweiger.

Some people criticize modeling. They say it's superficial and that it causes men and women to obsess over physical beauty. Well, you know, I was just at the mall this week, looking around. I don't think we're obsessing enough. You know, if you feel that Americans place too much emphasis on good looks, well then, I suggest that you go to the food court right there near Sears, and you stare at the unending Noah's Ark off-ramp of Ugly parading by with Stealth bomber–sized slices of Sbarro pizza dripping out of their three-toothed pieholes, and I guarantee you, you will sprint home and light a candle for Gia.

Of course, that's just my opinion, I could be wrong.

Wrestling

Now, I don't want to get off on a rant here, but for all its gritty, everyman appeal, pro wrestling exists in its own odd parallel universe, a world where bad guys are good guys, good guys are bad guys, there's more spandex than in Michael Flatley's overnight bag, and Dennis Rodman's ring name is "the Quiet Man."

Wrestling today fuses postpubescent rage with our overwhelming, deep-rooted sense of powerlessness and disappointment. Who am I bullshittin'? It's fun. It's bad, filthy American fun.

You know, I'd love to be able to sit down and watch wrestling with my kids, but so much of it now involves behavior that I don't want them emulating, like giving people the finger and yelling, "Kiss my ass!" I've told them time and time again, that is behavior which is only acceptable from Daddy when he's stuck in traffic.

What makes wrestling so attractive to the masses? Well, it embodies the age-old struggle of good vs. evil. Do you know how much more popular politics would be if the Senate solved its problems like professional wrestling matches? Wouldn't you love to see Ted Kennedy body-slamming Trent "the Rifleman" Lott over gun control? Or Bill "the President of Love" Clinton throwing rose petals and blowing kisses to the crowd after ramming Ken Starr's head into the knee of a Hispanic midget manning the turnbuckle?

One question that pops into people's minds when you mention professional wrestling is, of course, "Is it real?" And the answer to that is: "Yes, it is." I mean, how phony can it be if Don King isn't making any money off it?

And then there's female wrestling. Glistening, surgically enhanced Amazons with names like Tammy Lynn Bytch scissor-locking their scrappy little hearts out. If you've never had the pleasure, I suggest you tune in on a Monday night and watch how *real* women work out their problems. Far more entertaining than that gutless simp Ally McBeal? Yeah, you bet your ass it is! Have you seen Nicole Bass? Pull off her wig and call Austin, 'cause she's a man, baby!

Now, how does one become a professional wrestler? The easiest way is to go to Harvard. They've got a great program there, only no one seems to know much about it.

Professional wrestlers choose their noms de guerre with all the care of Bond villains. The names must be catchy, short, descriptive, and communicate the essential qualities of their character instantly. Sable. Sleek and powerful.

Hollywood Hulk Hogan. Flamboyant, massive, and powerful. Goldberg. Talmudic, non-pork–eating, won't wrestle on Yom Kippur, and powerful.

Years ago, I myself wrestled under the moniker Sarcasmoblaster. I would immobilize my adversaries by determining their psychological weak points and then hammering away at them with demeaning observations, until they finally became paralyzed with low self-esteem, allowing me to easily pin them for the win. I was doing great until some huge deaf guy kicked my ass.

Hey, let's put our cards on the canvas here. Pro wrestling involves an incredible amount of athleticism, but strictly speaking, I'm not quite sure it's a sport in the traditional sense. It's also entertainment. To call pro wrestling a sport is akin to calling the French loyal and brave, or Hillary Clinton a New Yorker.

Sure, it's easy to take the holier-than-thou route, and criticize pro wrestling for glamorizing violence, or selling T-shirts with an upraised middle finger and the words SUCK IT emblazoned on the front. But you know what? I choose not to go that route. I choose to look deeper, to see within pro wrestling a mirror for our own times, a mirror that, like all great works of art, forces us to probe our own troubled human natures. For who among us has not wrestled with the colorfully masked demons of self-doubt, trying to smash them with the folding chairs of daily routine, all the while dreading the pile driver of rejection?

So kudos to you, Diamond Dallas Page! Fight the good fight, Disco Inferno! Bravo to you, Buff Bagwell and Mr. Ass!

You make America great! God bless you all! And from the bottom of my heart, I salute you. Suck it, you magnificent bastards!

Of course, that's just my opinion, I could be wrong.

Special Interest Groups

You know what the biggest problem is with our country? Too many special interest groups. A bunch of whiny jag-offs whose core belief is: What's good for them must be good for all of us.

Now, I don't want to get off on a rant here, but it seems that the special interest groups have narrowed the stripes on Old Glory into a democracy-for-sale computer bar code. Do you realize it's almost as easy to buy a politician these days as it is to buy a semiautomatic rifle?

From the NRA to the AARP, any group with enough brains to slap a few initials together can have an influence on Congress.

In case you're not familiar with the way our political system works, our government is like a wild party and you and I are not invited. We pay for the party, but we can never go.

We send other people to the party for us, but once they get there, they tell us they can't get us in to the party, and we end up stuck behind the velvet rope with some mook named Joey G. from Staten Island.

Lobbyists exist in a world of polished loafers, golden handshakes, and hearty, conspiratorial laughs that chill you to the bone because, every time you hear one, you know another of your elected leaders has just been bought. With one swipe of their fat Mont Blanc pens, lobbyists erase the work of a thousand pulled levers behind a thousand sliding curtains.

What special interest groups are best at is magnifying their pinprick causes into yawning chasms of need. I hear the Lesbian Farmers of America want all silos taken down because they represent a phallocentric vision of American agriculture. Hey, sorry, but where else are we gonna store our seed?

You know, it appears that many of the most powerful special interest groups have a conservative bent.

That's because conservatives desire to make other people live the way they think they should live, as opposed to liberals, who think other people should live any way they want to as long as they don't wear fur.

You know, the competition for campaign contributions in Washington has resulted in a body of lawmakers who go about courting the support of special interest groups with all the restrained dignity of a wolverine on a Fatburger.

And it's probably going to be that way for a long time. Because the power to change the laws lies in the hands of politicians, the exact people who have the greatest stake in maintaining the status quo. You might as well appoint a crack addict as drug czar.

In Washington money not only talks, it walks, eats, sleeps, golfs, fishes, and goes to the Super Bowl. You can have access to any politician for a price. You might not be able to get tickets to see Springsteen, but if the money's right, I'm pretty sure you can get Al Gore to sing "Born to Run" at your kid's wedding.

Hey, I don't begrudge lobbyists their livelihood. Anybody willing to sit in a fancy restaurant for three hours watching Strom Thurmond trying to gum open a lobster tail is working hard for their money.

And truth be told, no matter what laws you pass to rid politics of big money, special interest groups will always figure out how to worm their way into the system because Congress will always be up for sale. That is why I propose we remove all pretense and simply turn the proceedings over to the good people from Sotheby's. Stand each congressman before a group of special interest lobbyists and just sell him to the highest bidder. Ladies and gentlemen of the tobacco industry, the next **lot** up for bid is Trent.

All kidding aside, folks, we have to figure out a way of stopping a small minority of highly organized zealots from beating the shit out of the rest of us just because we're all apathetic fuck-ups.

And if events of the last few months show us anything, we should start with the NRA. The NRA is notorious for sabotaging essentially decent lawmakers who want a little sanity in our nation's gun laws by showering their political opponents with money. And if the antigun politician doesn't have an opponent, the NRA will prop up some half-wit, nondescript right wing jerk-off with a bad toupee and a midnight cable access show and run him. Now, your voice in Congress is some guy in a forty-dollar suit whose brain, in ballistic terms, is a hollow-point, but that doesn't matter because all he's got to do is remember who took him to the dance when the floor calls for a vote to ban bazookas from church.

In watching the debates over gun control, I just have to sit back and admire the unique brand of effrontery displayed by the NRA. These guys are relentless at thumping away on the American Constitution to block even a child-proof lock on the trigger of a snub-nosed pistol, but at the same time, they turn a blind eye to the central tenet of that very Constitution, that the will of **we,** the people, must prevail.

We want the guns off the street. All of us, except the NRA. So if the whores in Congress would just tell us what their votes are fetching these days, I think all of us would be more than willing to cut the check and stop letting Moses, Magnum, and the rest of the NRA call all the shots around here.

Of course, that's just my opinion, I could be wrong.

Is Everything
Getting Worse?

Now, I don't want to get off on a rant here, but is everything getting worse? Well, it's hard to say. Of course we tend to romanticize the past. You know why? Because it's groovy, baby!

It's human nature to glorify the past and preserve it in our minds in a delicious, if inaccurate, candied haze. I mean, granted, at one time movies cost a buck and the ozone layer was intact. But you also have to remember that back then women and blacks were treated like dirt and you had to walk all the way across the room to change channels on the TV. I mean, it was fucking barbaric.

So let's see. On the one hand, the economy is booming and technology is a cornucopia from which new wonders constantly tumble. On the other hand, the world seems just as war-torn as ever, and the global environment is heating up faster than President Clinton watching Jennifer Lopez stoop over to pick up a quarter on the floor. That's why I believe we need to step back and ask the one single question that will allow us to accurately and objectively assess the true state of the world: How are things for Dennis Miller? And the answer is: Pretty good, thank you. So I guess the world's doing all right.

Seriously, are things really getting worse? Well, a pessimist might say that everything in the world is steadily going downhill—that nowadays, everything is shit. Well, call me a cockeyed optimist, but I don't think that's true. I think everything has always been shit . . .

Yes, there were some great movies or novels or politicians back in the old days, but we remember them precisely because everything they were surrounded by was shit. Most old movies? Shit. Most old novels? Shit. Most actors? Shit. Most rock music? Shit. Most shit? Shit.

I think it's safe to say that we're financially richer, but morally poorer, these days. We expect those in power to lie, we expect our contemporaries to cheat, and we expect our employees to steal. I'm not even the most cynical guy at parties anymore. It's usually some Amish coke dealer off in the corner, with a windmill-powered cellphone.

Yes, we have more gadgets in our houses to make our lives easier, but I'm spending half my life driving back to the store to ask them how these things work. Fucking shoelaces.

Sure, Americans are riding a wave of optimism. And I think that's all well and good. But I can't help but believe that all this good cheer stems primarily from an ever-increasing tendency to lower our standards. I mean, look at our choices for President. Gore vs. Bush? Hey, whoopee, let's all hop on the bland wagon there. Christ, I'd rather give Clinton a third term. At least it's fun to watch him wriggle out of the straitjacket after he gets caught putting the little head of state into some strange oval office.

Folks, here's the bottom line. It's naïve to think that some things aren't getting worse. Americans are hoarding guns while hiding behind bolted doors, feeling more suspicious of one another than ever before, as our nation's youth is contaminated by movies, games, and television that trivialize both sex and violence. So then, why is everyone feeling so damn good about everything? That's very easy. Cash, Prozac, and all the diamond-hard boners you can shake a prescription at.

Of course, that's just my opinion, I could be wrong.

Blatant Self-Promotion

Now, I don't want to get off on a rant here, but when it comes to blatant self-promotion these days, there is more desperate chest pounding going on than a twenty-four-hour "ER" marathon.

Today everyone is a celebrity: Cajun chefs, CEOs, transvestite hookers. Hey, we live in a world where even Mother Teresa had people.

I know in every business you have to sell yourself. I don't have a problem with that. But you have to know when to stop. There are people out there who are more overexposed than Edgar Winter slathered in baby oil lying on a bed of aluminum foil under a magnifying glass at high noon in Palm Springs.

Nowadays, even the average American has mastered the art of spin. I got a press release from my mailman today that included his head shot, outlined his views on stamp placement, and announced that his next project is delivering tomorrow's mail.

Donald Trump is the Donald Trump of self-promotion. What's with affixing his surname to anything he touches in life? The only thing the word "Trump" should be synonymous with is a really bad comb-over and eyebrows that are denser than the women he dates.

And then there's Dennis Rodman. Now, I have to say I used to be a fan of his, because when he hit the floor, he was the complete warrior and he left all of his freak-show bullshit in the pants pocket of his warm-up suit. But last season, that all changed. Dennis, if you happen to be watching tonight on a television set in the waiting room of whatever tattoo parlor you're in, I think one of your skull-piercings might've accidentally nicked the part of the brain that keeps you from buying into your own hype. So let's pull out all those hoops and loops and rings and car keys, bass lures, cotter pins, and paper clips, and let the holes heal back up so you can start doing some rebounding this season. 'Cause right now, you're on the verge of becoming the world's most passé wind chime.

Oh, and by the way, if there's anybody out there tonight who has not yet bought a tae-bo tape, please, I'm begging you, bite the bullet and send in your goddamn money. Because until you do, Billy Blanks is not going to leave any of us alone for a single fucking minute.

Hey, and look at Madonna. No, I mean, really, look at her . . . or she'll die.

Do you realize we actually have celebrities in this culture who are celebrities merely because they are celebrities? Melissa Rivers, Downtown Julie Brown, Mr. Blackwell. What exactly do these people do? Other than bemoan the travails of living in the fishbowl? You know something, you gotta hand it to Mary Jo Buttafuoco. At least she took a bullet in the face.

A word of warning, however, my nontalented friends: If you want to last beyond Flavor of the Month, you'd better make sure you can live up to your self-generated buzz, because it can get mighty lonely sitting there, thirty-five rows back next to Brigitte Nielsen at the Calvin Klein spring show, as she tries to pitch you *Red Sonja II.*

And don't ever take yourself so seriously that you refer to yourself in the third person. You know, the day I say, "Dennis Miller has to look out for Dennis Miller," I want you all to crown Dennis Miller the King of Assholia.

Truth be told, there are so many me-monkeys out there, they've actually cheapened our appreciation of true accomplishment. Cynics even grumbled that World Cup soccer player Brandi Chastain was guilty of blatant self-promotion when she dramatically ripped off her jersey after scoring the winning kick last year.

Well, I disagree. I say that what she did was well within the acceptable parameters of genuine emotional release. Let me tell you something, if that had been me out there, I would've de-pantsed myself and shouted "Take that, you spying Commie bastards!" while bending over to flash my naked, hairy, pivotal-goal-of-the-game-scorin' ass at their bench, and then everyone in that stadium would've gotten a long, lingering face-ful of my sweaty championship-winning balls as I took a prancing victory lap around the field screaming, "Bring on the cash, motherfuckers! Bring it on!"

Of course, that's just my opinion, I could be wrong.

Sex & Viagra

You know, love might make the world go round, folks, but sex certainly greases the poles.

Now, I don't want to get off on a rant here, but there's no greater pleasure known to man than sex. Right and true, sex can be a wonderful expression of love. Wrong and false, well, it's even better then, isn't it?

Which is not to say sex doesn't come with more strings attached than Geppetto's mistress. It is a slippery slope from "Trust me, baby, it won't get weird" to "It got weird, didn't it?"

The only other animals besides humans who have sex for fun as well as reproduction are dolphins and chimpanzees. And why not? They're great fucks . . . Or so I've heard.

Now, of course, the difference between us and the animals is, we have to explain sex to our kids, and everyone does it differently. A farmer explains it by comparing it to the way the crops are planted, a mechanic may use the example of nuts and bolts. Now, I'm a comedian, so I plan on hiring funnyman Buddy Hackett to explain it to my kids.

And believe me, kids need to know. I don't care what your hobby is before puberty hits, because as soon as it does, nature assigns you a new hobby. Let's just say when I was fourteen, I was treated for tennis elbow and I didn't even own a fucking racquet. Let he who has a free hand cast the first stone. I wasn't exactly subtle about my self-discovery, either. I put tiki torches all around my bed, a poster of Farrah Fawcett on my ceiling, and a spring-loaded tissue dispenser on my nightstand, and then I proceeded to work my own crank like it was the gearshift on a Volkswagen bus that I was trying to rock out of a fucking mud hole. Ah, the good old days . . . Last Thursday.

Yes, birds do it, bees do it, even married presidents in the Oval Office do it. You know what? We don't like people who don't look like they have sex. Kenneth Starr and Linda Tripp both had approval ratings lower than a fat dachshund's balls. But Bill Clinton . . . through the roof . . . Literally. And the reason Bill Clinton skated is because, underneath it all, we like the idea that he was getting some strange. I don't know what his presidential library will look like in Arkansas, but I bet out front, there's gonna be a big shooting fountain going off every twenty minutes or so.

We're fortunate to be living in a time when it's easier than ever before to explore your sexuality and enhance your lovemaking. But when it comes to sexual aids, be careful to follow the directions on the package. I used too much of that delay cream once and I'm still waiting for an orgasm from a drive-in movie handjob in August of '72.

And colored condoms don't do a thing for me. You see, I'm a winter and all those bright tones make me look washed out.

You know, there was a time when men dreaded getting old because they knew it would rob them of their sexual power. But thanks to modern medicine, couples are having sex well into their seventies and eighties, to the point where you can now buy edible panties fortified with calcium.

And now with the addition of the miracle drug Viagra, millions of men who were no longer able to have sex are banging away like monkeys with wooden spoons on lobster pots.

How does Viagra work? It's simple. Inside every one of those little blue pills is a miniaturized photo of a dripping wet Sophia Loren getting back on board the sponge boat in *Boy on a Dolphin*. Works every time.

I guess like all things in this era of unfettered capitalism, science and technology have turned human sexuality into yet another profit center. Between penile lengthening, Viagra, and boob jobs, doctors are nailing up shingles to get in on all the nailing going on. You got guys who haven't even been to medical school setting up shop in a kiosk on a traffic island on Sunset Boulevard who'll inject chicken fat into your dick for twenty bucks at a red light. Or ten bucks, if you've got the Entertainment 2000 coupon book.

Hey, civilizations come and go, but the one constant throughout the ages has been and always will be the orgasm. Rich man, poor man, beggar man, thief . . . I don't care what your social stratum is. When that climax lightning bolt comes roaring down your loins, there's only one thing on your mind: Why in the hell is everybody else on this bus starin' at me?

Of course, that's just my opinion, I could be wrong.

America's Fascination with Rebels

Now, I don't want to get off on a rant here, but I happen to find it a source of endless amusement that in 2000 America, the most effective way to insinuate oneself into the gooey embrace of the mainstream is by becoming a rebel.

Now, what exactly is a rebel? Sid Vicious was a rebel, but so was Rosa Parks when she sat in the front of the bus—probably because she saw Sid Vicious sitting in the back.

And while rebels come in all shapes and sizes, rebellion is still essentially a function of youth. If you're still rebelling in your late thirties, well, trust me, someone's paying you a big fat shitload of money to do it.

Now, I know there are a couple of teenagers who watch my TV show, who see my goatee, who hear me utter the occasional f-word and assume that I am a fucking rebel. Let me clue you in on a little secret, kids. I get paid to do this.

I'm about as rebellious as the triangle player in KC and the Sunshine Band during contract negotiations. You know, if I really were a rebel, I'd be on a live public access call-in show right now with Dr. Guine, a vegan chiropractor from Costa Mesa. As a matter of fact, I am so not a rebel, if HBO wanted me to start every show by singing "It's Raining Men," well, then you better break out the hip waders.

You know, for all of our corn-fed, button-down, shopping-mall conformity, we Americans owe our very identity to a proud tradition of rebellion. I mean, look at the Pilgrims. Dressed all in black, facial hair on the men, no makeup on the women.

Give 'em shades and a clove cigarette and they're every spoken-word coffeehouse performer you've ever walked out on. The Pilgrims were rebelling against what they felt were oppressive figures of religious authority. So they got on a boat, established a colony in the New World, and became . . . oppressive figures of religious authority.

Our contemporary rebels take their cue from rock & roll, and whether it was Jerry Lee Lewis humping his piano or Elvis Presley humping absolutely everything else, that Devil music turned out to be the bent paperclip that unlocked America's chastity belt.

There was no greater slap to my wide-eyed adolescent face than learning Mick Jagger had attended the London

School of Economics. Although I'm sure the theories of supply and demand came in handy after he hooked up with Keith.

You see, what makes our culture simultaneously infuriating and gratifying is its uncanny ability to muzzle the rebel by gradually absorbing him into the system with an intoxicating web of money, fame, and chicks that ultimately dulls his senses to the point where he can no longer even remember what it was he was fucking rebelling against in the first place. Never forget: The ultimate rebel, the homosexual beat junkie writer William Burroughs, who penned some of the most corrosive literature of the twentieth century, ended up doin' Nike commercials to pay for his naked lunch. I think the shoe was the Heroin Jordan model, if I'm not mistaken?

Or take a look at the phenomena of tattooing and body piercing. At the very beginning of the nineties, these were two can't-miss methods of ensuring you instant cool as well as the wrath of your family and employers. Now, I believe genital piercing is covered by Blue Cross/Blue Sack and the main drag of Anytown, U.S.A., boasts a tattoo parlor between Starbucks and . . . the other Starbucks.

You know, we're guilty of romanticizing rebels in film. But unlike in the movies, in real life, most of them aren't working because they've pissed off every boss they ever had, because they can only get rebellious in the workplace, seeing as they live in a converted laundry room in their parents' basement. The only machine these losers rage against has WHIRLPOOL printed on the front of it.

You know, you'd probably have to go back to the era of the Vietnam war to find a place where true rebellion lived in the soul of a generation. But I'm sure that by now even the most ardent protesters of the war don't consider themselves American rebels as much as just plain old everyday Canadian citizens.

I used to have a theory that every generation rebelled against the generation before it. But then I found out every generation, like the one before it, just likes to get wasted and fuck and the older generation gets pissed off because they have to work and they can't get wasted and fuck anymore.

In the end, that's the problem with a lot of rebels. They believe that with freedom comes a lack of responsibility. Well, you know, it's fine to be the lone wolf who breaks away from the pack, but you gotta walk a fine line between being an individualist and just being really, really annoying. Okay?

Come on, people, *fight the power! Be different,* 'cause, you know, don't you want to fit in?

Of course, that's just my opinion, I could be wrong.

Taxes

Now, I don't want to get off on a rant here, but the American tax system is more complicated than a prenup between Bill Gates and Marla Maples. The current tax code is harder to understand than Bob Dylan reading *Finnegans Wake* in a wind tunnel.

I find it awfully ironic that just a short couple of centuries after our plucky forebears heaved the Tetley's into Boston Harbor in outrage over the few cents' worth of taxes they had to kick back to Crumpetland, every April we Americans now meekly fork over a king's ransom to keep our huge, lumbering, Tarkus-like democracy creaking along.

Now personally, my taxes are a fucking nightmare. I require more extensions than Yanni. And what puzzles and frustrates me so much is how inconsistent the tax code is. For instance, why does the IRS let one person check the "clergy" box and not get in trouble, and then come down hard on someone else who might technically not be a minister, but through his weekly live talk show on HBO brings just as much comfort to the masses? It's unfair, brothers and sisters. It's the Devil's work.

Throughout history, we have all felt put upon by the tax man. But even Jesus said, "Render unto Caesar what is Caesar's. Render unto God what is God's." It's easy for Jesus to say. He never paid a dime in taxes because his accountant, Morty Glick, was a fucking genius.

Of course, if you don't want to pay for a real accountant, you can always go to one of those tax prep places where you'll be entrusting your fiscal future to some part-time H&R Blockhead who's on sabbatical from his regular gig teaching a Shetland pony grooming for singles class at the Learning Annex. Quite frankly, I've seen more financial acumen watching my dog swallow a nickel.

And of course, no discussion of taxes would be complete without invoking the IRS. You know the IRS, those sons of . . . liberty and fairness. I can't say enough about the brave men and women who maintain and replenish the coffers of the Republic with unswerving dedication. I have nothing but praise for these secular saints who have gone unheralded far too long. Others may criticize the IRS, but not I. Not Dennis Miller of Los Angeles, California. Social Security number 873-82-2889.

Maybe instead of taxes, the government should simply charge us for their services item by item. I propose that each year you get a checklist from the Feds, then you mark off what you used and pay accordingly. You know, like the mini-bar in your hotel room. Only far less expensive. For Christ's sake, even the Pentagon wouldn't have the audacity to charge twelve bucks for a bag of pistachios. And while we're on the subject, Mr. Marriott, can you make that metal clasp on top of the jelly bean jar just a little more difficult to operate? All right? This thing's harder to get off than Martha Stewart on a set of dirty sheets.

Anyway, maybe the reason government is so expensive is the capital is in Washington, where a cup of coffee costs three bucks. The overhead is killing us. We should run our government more like a contemporary American corporation. Move the capital to Jakarta and have our laws made by eight-year-old kids earning six cents a day. C'mon, just do it!

For too long, our elected officials have treated our tax money like a bowl of M&Ms on a receptionist's desk that they can keep grabbing handfuls from any time they want. It has to stop. They need to be accountable. So from now on, any time they spend something, I want to see a fucking receipt.

Hey, I would gladly pay more taxes if I could be guaranteed that my money is going toward the greater public good. The thing that sticks in my craw about giving my tax money to the government is: I know that some slimy jag-off in Congress is gonna wind up on a junket to Bora Bora sunning his fat ass on my dime.

Look, the tax code is an atonal collection of discordant notes tapped out by the eighteen-carat-gold-ring-wearing fingers of five thousand special interest weasels in a grabby cluster-fuck that would give nightmares to even Clive Barker. Every bizarre exemption, every deduction that wouldn't apply to you in ten million years is there for one reason—and one reason alone: to save money for some pig lobbyist who then kicks back a portion of it to some scumbag politician's campaign war chest. I say we eliminate the middleman and lend some dignity to the process. Every April 16, strip each congressman buck naked, dip them in honey, then give them sixty seconds to roll around in the tax revenues, and let them keep whatever sticks to their bloated, liver-spotted carcasses, and then guess what? We get to keep the rest.

Of course, that's just my opinion, I could be wrong.

Paranoia

ow, I don't want to get off on a rant here, but America has become more paranoid than Ross Perot watching *Three Days of the Condor* after a seventy-two-hour crack binge.

You know, the word "paranoia" is a clinical term describing the feeling of imminent annihilation by a dark conspiratorial force. I believe in right wing politics, it's known as "vision."

Are you paranoid? Yeah, you. When you leave work, do you think people move your stuff and then put it back exactly where it was? More to the point, did you just react to that question by saying, "How does he know that about me?"

Hey, I believe we live in a time where it's all right to be a little paranoid. With sweeping technological advances that permit spy satellites to spot precancerous moles on our inner thighs, it has become increasingly evident that the only way to not feel you're being watched is by starring in a sitcom on UPN.

Be that as it may, no one has greater faith in Man's innate goodness than yours truly. From the time my lead-reinforced Brinks truck drops me off inside this heavily fortified studio bunker, sixty floors below HBO World Headquarters, to the time my tenth-degree red-belt manservant Drago tucks me in and I fall asleep inside my titanium vault, watching *Ice Station Zebra* on a perpetual loop, well, I am just brimming with nothing but trust in my fellow man's commitment to the higher good.

You know what makes me paranoid? People who say, "Oh, you're just being paranoid." Actually, I have performer's paranoia. I worry that Jay Leno's phone is more tapped than mine.

If you want to see just how paranoid our culture has become, then take a cybercruise down the information Highway 51 known as the Internet. What is it about the Internet that draws the paranoid like Asian businessmen to blonde lap dancers?

Well, the World Wide Web provides a lushly fertile petri dish in which sweaty paranoia and wacky conspiracy theories thrive like a dose of clap at a biker rally.

With a few strokes on a keyboard, you can hook up with fellow crackpots who will not only concur with your theory that President Clinton faked a knee injury to cover having his dick straightened at Bethesda Naval Hospital by the renowned Flemish dick straightener Dr. Claude Ballz.

Conspiracy theories come from a natural human desire to see the world as an ordered place. If everything bad that happens to you is the result of a complicated plot involving the Freemasons, the Rockefellers, and Joey Lawrence, you become the center of the universe. But if you bump into a guy in a bar and he beats the crap out of you not because he is a subagent sent by the Trilateral Commission on behalf of the Illuminati but merely because he drives a pickup truck with a bumper sticker that reads: SHIT HAPPENS . . .

Well, in that case, you realize that you are just a single random Ping-Pong ball in the great lottery popper that we call life.

So why are we paranoid? Well, looking nervously over our shoulder, we see that our generation was shaped by paranoid men like Richard Nixon and suspicious women like J. Edgar Hoover.

Therefore, when it comes to paranoia, most folks train their night-vision goggles on the federal government. And I admit, every time I butt heads with government buttheads, I get the feeling it's personal, too. But I'm made more paranoid by corporations: car companies that lie about their safety records; chemical firms selling toxic weed killers that wind up in our food—you never see Scully and Mulder take on these guys because, quite frankly, these guys advertise on the fucking "X-Files."

Come on, really, let's face it. The idiots in Washington, D.C., can't even investigate a conspiracy let alone create one. Do you really think Al D'Amato could be in charge of anything other than the flavor of the pudding cup in his lunch box and keep quiet about it? D'Amato would be panicking like Barney Fife at Iwo Jima.

You know, conspiracy has always been a part of American life. And why not? It makes us feel more important to think we're special enough for the infamous "they" to take the time to put one over on us. Hey, the biggest conspiracy has always been the fact that there is no conspiracy. No one's out to get you. No one even gives a shit whether you live or die. There. You feel better now?

Of course, that's just my opinion, I could be wrong.

Network News

ow, I don't want to get off on a rant here, but the line between news and entertainment has become a border so often crossed, it makes Brownsville, Texas, look like Cold War Berlin. But if you don't mind, I'd like my news with a little more substance than my dream I had last night about the lactating leprechaun. Okay?

All the network evening news shows are exactly alike. An interchangeable animatronic anchor and thirty minutes of the same big blur: Who's Clinton shagging, what'd my stocks do, look how crazy those foreigners are, and I can't believe that squirrel can actually water-ski. And because of that similarity, the only way for them to differentiate themselves is by drawing deeper and deeper from the should-be off-limits wellspring of human pain and suffering. And in doing so, TV journalists have become nothing more than millionaire carnival barkers with good diction and so much hair spray on, they make Margaret Thatcher look like Tori Amos.

And while we're on the subject of stiff, could there be a more appropriate moniker in the business than Stone Phillips? This guy makes Mount Rushmore look like a fucking episode of "The Monkees."

But all criticisms aside, there's still no denying the clear demarcation between national network news and local news programs. If network news is crap, local news is crap concentrate.

First of all, just the basic production values on some of these programs give a hint as to the quality of their content. The cheap, fluorescent lighting creates all the warmth of a porn-shoot in a K-Mart, while the ever-present tacky sky blue background is always the exact color of the rented tuxedo you wore to your sexless prom in 1976.

Local news will entice you with uplifting fare like an eight-part series on the special challenges facing immigrant midgets, then some Sears undie model with a cutesy name, like Kent Tsunami or Stormy Wetdry, comes in to do the weather, before throwing it back to some Hitler Youth anchor clone, who, if teeth were brains, would rule the planet.

You know, if Velveeta ever morphs into a human form, it will become a local newscaster. I like watching these nozzleheads try to give some depth and insight to the news stories. They get that same blank expression on their face as my dog does when I put him on the phone.

In L.A., there are about six to eight different news shows every night, all vying for your attention with the exact same story. Their helicopters are stacked on top of each other like a sleeve of Ritz crackers and you can use the remote at home like a director trying to get all sorts of different camera angles on the Malibu mud slides. You know what I think causes mud slides? The vibrations from fucking helicopters, okay?

The I-Team investigative story is also known for drumming up high local ratings. Especially when the overzealous Anglo member of the I-Team Krazy Glues his eyes back and goes undercover in a Chinese restaurant kitchen to tell you that it's not all that clean. Hey, guess what? We know it's not an operating theater back there, but we like the food anyway. Okay? So shut up, before they start raising the prices to buy new mops.

Now, the scary teaser is one tactic news stations use to lure viewers. Reporting some infinitesimal possibility of a terror in your home that you don't know about. Is there a deadly microbe in your kids' milk? Tune in tonight at six o'clock and find out. Hey, what about the milk our kids are drinking between now and six o'clock? Okay? Could you maybe cut into "She's the Sheriff" and give us a little preview from the poison center on that one, Sparky McDowner?

And then, there's the local news trump card, the high-speed freeway chase. Now sure, I know that the only thing more inane than trying to outrun a squadron of police cruisers running at warp speed in a four-cylinder lime green '71 Gremlin is actually watching it and taping it to watch again until Fox puts it out on laserdisc, but isn't that really what television news is all about? The sudden realization that we, the voyeuristic viewers, are no better than they, the gratuitous gatekeepers? And they're no better than we are?

That all of us, you, me, Carol Anne, Mike, Rock with the sports, and Flip with the weather, are all participating in a big pseudo-journalistic circle jerk? Huh? The networks get rich, and we—we are temporarily reassured that there are lives way more fucked up than ours. Sounds like a pretty fair deal to me.

Look, I'm all for making money. But just don't call it the news. Because it's not. You'd see a tighter grip on reality watching Michael Jackson preening in front of a fun house mirror than you do watching television news. So don't call it news. Let's call it what it is. Let's call it "The Six O'Clock Shit Thankfully Not Happening to You."

Of course, that's just my opinion, I could be wrong.

Talk Radio

Now, I don't want to get off on a rant here, but up and down America's radio dial today, you're likely to hear about as much rational discourse as you would watching Charles Manson and Charles Nelson Reilly trying to put together a bicycle on Christmas morning. Marconi has got to be oscillating in his grave.

If talk radio proves anything, it's that humans sitting in traffic would rather listen to Fran Drescher screaming the Sanskrit alphabet than be left alone with their own thoughts.

All this being said, I love talk radio. Where else can the entire situation in China be summed up with the simplistic generalization: "Jang Zemin is a jag-off"? You know, other than, of course, my show.

You know, we used to listen to music in our cars to relax. Now we love to eavesdrop on submutants arguing over psychotic deal points and having their fights refereed by an embittered host who used to spin records on the A.M. station in Utica, New York, from where, he constantly reminds us, he got fired by "the suits" for refusing to play "Mandy." Don't enter into the morning zoo unless your backpack's fully loaded, *mi amigo*.

As a matter of fact, getting a radio talk show in America appears to be easier than Caribbean Med School. All you need is a mouth that works and an audience that doesn't.

Hey, the only thing greater than America's love affair with talk radio is the love affair the hosts seem to have with themselves. And no one is more full of himself, or, for that matter, more full, than Rush Limbaugh. Limbaugh articulates the blindingly white anger of every short-sleeved Wal-Mart assistant manager in America who's outraged because a black kid called him by his first name.

Now, quite frankly, I don't have all that much to say about Rush Limbaugh, because Al Franken already wrote a book that cut him into ten million pieces, each of which weighed roughly half a pound.

Limbaugh is emblematic of what's wrong with the medium. It rarely educates, but only reinforces and reaffirms the narrow-minded prejudices of both host and listener. Let's face it, only somebody who already believes that sunlight is an international conspiracy is going to listen to a program called "Dr. Gary Grimm's Sunlight Is an International Conspiracy Show."

I RANT

Many talk radio hosts are so misinformed, and play so fast and loose with the truth, they make *Mein Kampf* read like *The Farmer's Almanac*. I've been berated by homeless squeegee guys who have a better line of reasoning.

That said, there are many programs being broadcast today that help people from all walks of life, with all types of problems. Personally, I like listening to "Car Talk with Click and Clack," the Tappet brothers. It's not only entertaining, but informative. Like when my cousin Ace and I rebuilt the 396 in my '68 El Camino. We bored the cylinders 30 over, put in a hotter cam, and topped it all off with a duo of Holley double-pumpers perched on a high-rise manifold. While we were at it, we tweaked the Turbo-400 tranny, popped in a low-ratio rear end, and stitched all that torque to the asphalt with a new set of Mickey Thompson 50 series comp street meat. Well, I don't have to tell you, we expected that sumbitch to light up like a Christmas tree and flat-out walk the dog. But it didn't. No matter what we tried, we couldn't get it to crack 16 in the quarter. Then we called "Car Talk." Turns out the new orange shag carpet I'd put on the floor was so thick it was keeping the cool "barefoot" gas pedal I'd installed from going all the way down! Thanks, Click! And thanks, Clack! You guys fucking rock, man!

Without a doubt, the most irritating format on talk radio today is the drive-time psychiatry show ... thirty-second diagnoses for thirty-year-old problems. Callers with maladies ranging from manic depression to chronic masturbation seek the wisdom of an oracle whose pool of psychiatric knowledge is filled by the tributaries of eighteen credit hours assisting in the Overdose Tent at the Pomona County Fair. By the way, in listening to these programs, I've noticed that chronic masturbators always seem to call in on a speaker phone.

Now, Dr. Laura Schlessinger is the current top dog, or should I say the alpha bitch, of the high-frequency shrink pack. Dr. Laura, a shrieking harpy with all the compassion of Charlie Starkweather with a thorn in his paw, harangues her listeners to be strong, stop whining, behave, don't be a slut, wise up, and stand on your own two feet.

Hey, thanks for the comforting insight, Doc, and oh, sorry about that house falling out of the sky onto your sister. With three books published which she endlessly hypes and a nationally syndicated talk show, Dr. Laura heads a virtual one-shrew empire and yet has the gall to tell women that if they work they're bad mothers. Well, let me ask you this, Aimee Simple McPherson, howzabout settin' an example by prying your bony digits off the lucrative business end of that microphone you're sitting behind and putting a sock in your pie hole? Hey, listeners, you wanna know what the first step in taking charge of your own life is? Hang up on Dr. Fucking Laura, okay?

Of course, that's just my opinion, I could be wrong.

The Space Program

You know something? I'm sick of technological advances. And I'm sick of that space shuttle taking off more frequently than Strom Thurmond has to pee.

Now, I don't want to get off on a rant here, but in post–Cold War America, isn't the space program a quaint relic of a bygone era? A time when two hostile superpowers competed to see who could launch a bigger rocket that would penetrate deeper and last longer, thrusting farther and farther into the yielding, virginal, mysterious depths of the fickle, man-eating bitch that was outer space.

Now, whether or not you feel the space program was worth the money, you have to admit: Astronauts are genuine heroes, no joke here, men and women so brave they make Edmund Hillary look like Shaggy from "Scooby-Doo." When it comes to astronauts, the word "hero" pops up as readily as a Bob Seger song on a strip club jukebox. Anybody who would strap themselves onto a giant deodorant spray can, set off a series of explosions under their ass until they've been blasted into the icy vacuum of deep space, and then step outside to take a walk must have more balls than a twenty-four-hour Tokyo driving range.

Growing up, I was enthralled by these brave men who risked their lives to explore the universe: Alan Shepard, Gus Grissom, John Glenn, Buzz Aldrin, Tony Nelson, Major Healy . . .

But that was over thirty years ago. Do you realize a third of us weren't even alive yet to watch Neil Armstrong leave the most recognizable footprint this side of Bruno Magli?

Personally, my biggest hero had to be Armstrong and I thank him for bringing out the latent patriot in me. Because when he planted that flag in the Sea of Tranquillity, well, I'll tell you, I was weeping like Richard Simmons at Streisand's wedding.

I also admired him because I know if the entire planet were hanging on the very first words I uttered after setting foot onto the moon, I would have screamed, "Who's the loser now, Susie Cooperman? Who's the loser now? Why don't you kiss my moon-walking ass, baby?"

The fact is, the space program was originally fueled by the desire to beat the Communists. Well, now that Russia's run by a Slavic version of W. C. Fields and it's 2.2 trillion pesos to the ruble, I mean, isn't our continued obsession with conquering the heavens the political equivalent of piling on? You know what? We've won. The Russians aren't going to the moon unless they climb there on a stack of empties.

In fact, America's space program, even in its current downsized condition, runs like a Lamborghini when compared to the Tom Joad shitwagon that is the Russian space program. As a matter of fact, I am beginning to think that *Mir* is the Russian word for "duct tape." This thing is so low-rent, the only thing that's missing is a pink flamingo and a clothes dryer on the porch.

Hey, at best, our space program is mankind's boldest effort to explore the universe. At worst, it is just another bloated government spending project, except with NASA, you can actually *watch* your money disappear into thin air.

And this is not to say I'm not appreciative of some of the peripheral benefits to space exploration. Listen, I'm as grateful as the next guy for the daily miracle that is Tang, but the fact is, if you spend billions and billions of dollars on *any* massive project, you're bound to come up with some by-products. So why not use that money to cure cancer and see if maybe space flight just happens to spin off from that breakthrough? Huh? What about that, Mr. Peabody?

Hey, exploring the universe is a laudable goal, but even if the Martian Land Rover beamed back a picture of God struggling with the childproof cap on a bottle of Mylanta, I'm not sure what we paid for that cosmic Kodak moment wouldn't have been better spent on a couple of thousand new inner-city math teachers.

I mean, if you want to observe a bleak, dust-covered, rock-strewn landscape with no detectable signs of life, can't you just buy a bus ticket to Bakersfield, for Christ's sake?

You want to know something? Boosting our knowledge of the cosmos is great for our self-esteem. And I think we should go back to it somewhere down the line. But right now, this planet is going to hell in a handbasket and I think we ought to just take a breather. I believe the next great breakthrough in space travel will probably come from some ubernerd who's germinating out there right now and will someday make a quantum leap and instantaneously transport us to the next level while doodling on a "Far Side" notepad.

But, you know something, I hope we never end up actually making contact with alien life-forms. Okay, let's suppose there is life elsewhere in this solar system. Do you have any idea of how fucked we'd be if they're anything like us? Well, if you don't, just head down to your local casino tonight and ask the American Indian who's dealing you blackjack about how much fun it is to meet new friends from faraway places.

Of course, that's just my opinion, I could be wrong.

The Backlash Against the Wealthy

You know, nobody gives the wealthy a bad name like "the Barely Adequate Gatsby," Donald Trump. But I'm not sure that Trump is an accurate representation of all affluent people. As a matter of fact, Donald Trump is to great wealth what John Wayne Gacy was to great art.

Now, I don't want to get off on a rant here, but lunch-pail America's current relationship with the rich is so complicated, it makes the ending of *2001* look like the burnt pie episode of "Mama's Family." There's a backlash against wealthy people in this country, ironically a country built on the belief that anyone and everyone can get as rich as they want to if they work hard enough, and the aforementioned backlash is gaining momentum like Roger Ebert snowboarding down a double black diamond trail.

Now, truth be told, lurking deep inside the id-infested batcave of every human psyche is the unspoken belief that each and every one of us deserves to be obscenely rich, right now! And that whoever got there before we did must have cheated. Therefore our interior monologue regarding the wealthy is more fragmented than the liner notes from *Quadrophenia* being read under a strobe light.

Look, the rich aren't all that different from anyone else. They just happen to drive better cars, live in bigger houses, have cooler stuff, and sleep with more attractive people than the rest of us. So why all the ill will?

As someone who has paid his dues by putting in many many grueling eight-hour work weeks and has amassed a modest pile of green purchasing rectangles myself, I wouldn't say I'm rich. Rather, I prefer to think of myself as superduper middle class.

Now, now, perhaps you're thinking it's blatantly self-serving for a defense of the rich to come from me, Dennis Pierpont Bouvier Miller III. You might think, in your quaint proletarian way, that my vast holdings in the famed Miller family fruitbat guano empire have caused me to lose touch with the people. But nothing could be further from the truth! From the moment I sit down at my rhino-tusk-inlayed breakfast table and ask Hasbro, my personal cereal-scooper, to serve me some Beluga Flakes, to the moment my long-time driver . . . Driver Guy . . . takes me to work, I'm always thinking about how to reinvent capitalism into an economic model that appeals to man's higher calling and sense of charity and community, because deep in my heart, I realize, if I did so, I could really make a shitload of money.

Now, whatever America as a whole might think, I am not afraid to come out and say it: I love the rich. I'm glad they have more money than I do. In most instances, I believe, they earned it. I realize this is a brave stand to take. I know you face incredible risks whenever you take the side of the wealthy and powerful against the poor and the dispossessed. But some hard truths must be spoken. Even though I'm fully aware of the danger involved in embedding my lips so deep into the ass of the Forbes 400, I'm going to look like an anteater with collagen injections.

And the rich guy I love the most is Bill Gates. Just look at him. Haircut with plastic safety scissors. How many billions is he worth and he's still hittin' the irregular Ban-Lon table in the middle of the aisle at Wal-Mart. Can you imagine what an unending carnival of wedgies his adolescence must have been? Is there anyone in the world who looks forward to high school reunions more than Bill Fucking Gates? Huh?

Well, I say, "God bless him." God bless Bill Gates. Look, maybe Bill Gates is an impossibly rich geek, but he's amassed his fortune by performing a valuable service to mankind: crushing other geeks.

But now with the Justice Department scrutinizing Gates the way a stoner eyes a box of Girl Scout Thin Mint cookies, you've got to wonder if the Feds are really out to shut down his alleged monopoly or just get their own piece of the silicon pie. Because, you see, ofttimes bringing down the rich is nothing more than a clever ruse to make new people rich.

Look, don't get me wrong, a bohemian approach to life has its place . . . *Bohemia!* I've been broke more in my life than I've had money, and when I was broke I had kinda convinced myself that I was a cool can't-be-bought idealist, tooling around in my rusted-out primer-colored Plymouth Valiant that had all the directional stability of a twenty-year-old shopping cart being pushed by Crispin Glover wearing an eye patch. In my own ketchup soup days, I used to somehow tell myself that the clueless moron who pulled up next to me at a light, blabbing into the cell phone of his Porsche Targa Carrera convertible was just being pathetic in his vain attempt to compensate for the lack of anything of real value in his shallow existence. And that he was really missing out on the deeper, more meaningful experiences in life like the one I had staying up last night counting out change from my Hills Brothers coffee can that was sitting on a dresser made from cinder blocks next to my futon, so I could buy Ramen noodles for breakfast. But I was just bullshitting myself, because I wanted to be rich, too.

Listen. No one should feel guilty about wanting more money. If you don't like it, well, sorry, comrade. Because complaining about this country's obsession with getting rich is like stepping onto a baseball diamond and bitching that nobody's playin' soccer. Trying to get rich is our national pastime. So pick up a bat, baby, and start swingin'. Because let's face it, folks, in this country we are all sailboats, and money is wind, and with enough of it, well, you can just about get blown anywhere.

Of course, that's just my opinion, I could be wrong.

Affirmative Action

ffirmative action. Stay with me, folks. This subject is tougher to sort through than Marv Albert's laundry.

Now, I don't want to get off on a rant here, but thirty-odd years ago affirmative action definitely had its place in this country because when it came to hiring practices, minorities had a harder time getting through the door than Brando coming out of an airplane bathroom. As a matter of fact, let's not mince around here.

In the history of this planet, no one group has inflicted more barbaric oppression on other groups than the white man. Ah, the white man. *Pastius suppressus.* Immediately after landing on these shores and tying up their boats, white European explorers' first instinct was to round up the quaint locals and force them to do the grunt work.

With that blueprint in place, for many years white Americans continued to do the wrong thing by playing a continent-wide game of keepaway with the good life. And anybody who tells you that racism is a thing of the past has his head buried deeper in the sand than an armless clamdigger.

All that being said, affirmative action cannot be the solution to our problems. Now, before you raise your pen to paper to demand my head, let me ask you this. Surely you're not insisting that individuals be given preferential treatment, based solely on the color of their skin. And certainly, you're not going to advance the position that minorities aren't as qualified as everybody else and need the booster chair to sit up at the big table. No, of course not. I didn't think so. Nobody's misguided enough to sell that wrongheaded spiel nowadays.

And that's exactly why affirmative action is a mistake. It works on the theory that what you are is more important than who you are, while slyly reinforcing the hideous notion that women and minorities can never advance without special permission.

Sure, I realize affirmative action was intended as a compensatory push to help fix the pendulum at a fair and equal center point, but more often than not in this country, when a good intention becomes institutionalized, the end result is further off the mark than the Boston Pops doing a Motorhead tribute album.

Affirmative action, left unchecked for the last thirty years, has resulted in one of the greatest plagues of our millennium. Yes. That's right. Vanilla Ice.

Now, it's true, I've never felt the numbing sting of knowing my application for a job was put in a different pile, my

I RANT

request for a bank loan was specially dog-eared, or a prospective landlord passed on me after peering through the peephole of the apartment I was hoping to rent. But I can't imagine that being accepted merely because of my race would sit with me any better than being denied because of it.

Now, being against affirmative action doesn't mean I am for discrimination. No sir, not one bit. I detest discrimination in all its forms and have tailored my writing staff accordingly. I have a skirt, a Spanish guy, a couple of Jews, and the rest are normal people, just like me.

But don't tell me I don't know what it's like to experience discrimination. For many years I was on the outside looking in until a court order forced HBO to institute hiring quotas for cynical little pricks.

Hey, it's up to us to decide if we want to live and work within a system that's based on merit or based on guilt. And while "diversity in the workplace" is certainly a desirable and noble goal, isn't "qualified people doing a good job in the workplace" even more important?

Wouldn't it make more sense to level the playing field when it can really do some good and give everybody the same opportunities at the *beginning* of the game instead of midway through? Christ, have you taken a look at an inner-city public school lately? Why not take all the time, money, and effort that's being misused on filling employment and university quotas and put them into ensuring that every little tadpole out there gets to make the same-sized splash in the job pond?

C'mon, should the son of a wealthy black businessman really be admitted to a law school over the equally qualified son of a white cab driver? No. Neither one should get in; this country already has enough goddamn lawyers as it is.

I'm sorry, but the bottom line is if I'm doing seventy-five mph on the freeway and I have to stop suddenly, I'm not wondering if a disabled black female Hispanic made my brakes, I'm wondering if they're gonna fucking work. Okay?

And when I put my life in the hands of a doctor, I want the person who scored the highest on the tests, did the best research, and knows what they're doing. I don't care if they're Black, White, Male, or Female. As long as they're Asian.

Of course, that's just my opinion, I could be wrong.

Hypochondria

Now, I don't want to get off on a rant here, but an increasing number of people seem to be exhibiting identical symptoms: uncontrollable whining, ceaseless complaining, and persistent worrying. Concerned medical experts have diagnosed this problem as an epidemic outbreak of . . . yes, that's right, hypochondria, the all-in-your-head cold.

Now, like the Supreme Court's description of pornography, hypochondria is impossible to define, but you know it when you see it. It's a collection of real and imagined symptoms that add up to the fact that you are more obsessed with your health than Humbert Humbert would be with Marsha Brady.

Hypochondria is essentially an upper-middle-class disease. You rarely see a poor guy blowing a paycheck on a specialist because he thinks the crisscross pattern he got on the backs of his legs from sitting on lawn furniture is the flesh-eating bacteria.

Despite nearly two thousand years of medical knowledge, doctors have yet to come up with a fix for hypochondria. And really why should they? It's easy money. They have as much motivation to cure hypochondria as Peter Tork does to cure nostalgia.

Those who are not worried about their health would say that hypochondriacs have their heads up their ass. Well, of course they do—because they're checking for polyps.

Now, one easy way to gauge this boy who cried Epstein-Barr epidemic is to peruse your local magazine kiosk. You've got *Health, Men's Health, Women's Health, Michael Jackson's Health, Prime Health, Natural Health, Alternative Health,* and the newest one, *"Hey, Jimmy, What's That on Your Face?"* These magazines lure their neurotic reader base into the psychosomatic tent with teaser headlines like: SITTING OR STANDING, WHICH IS WORSE?; TOOTHPASTE, THE SILENT KILLER; and WHY YOU MUST NEVER BLINK AGAIN.

Another cause of hypochondria is the demystification of medicine. Doctors used to be these godlike figures who came down from Mount Stethoscope to cure our afflictions with their Hippocratic magic. But now, with a cure for most common illnesses on the supermarket shelves right next to the Slim Jims, any shithead who gets "Quincy" on cable thinks he could've saved the world with a pipe cleaner and some baking soda.

Personally, I take exception to the label "hypochondriac." I prefer to think of myself as spectacularly self-absorbed. I have been to so many doctors' offices for the past thirty years that I can identify the tribe of naked Pygmies in *National Geographic* by the color plate in their lips. Sure I wash my hands fifty times a day. But that's not because I'm afraid of catching a cold. I just can't get them clean. Really. I did something horribly, horribly wrong, many years ago, and I can't get them clean . . .

My wife and I have a simple system to deal with what she calls "my problem." I tell her I'm not feeling well and she tells me to shut the fuck up.

Of course, I'm not alone. Talking about our ailments has become a national pastime, more popular than going to the movies, playing baseball, or blowing the President while he eats a piece of apple pie.

But just because we all kvetch about our health to one degree or another, it doesn't make it right. Let's face it, life is a gift even more fleeting than the career of the Fine Young Cannibals. And you can't enjoy the ride if you're constantly checking the dashboard for warning lights.

But there are some definite signs that you might be a hypochondriac. Like if your medical ID bracelet says: EVERYTHING. Or if you feel fine and then worry that your complete and utter lack of symptoms is the first sign of an incredibly rare medical condition called Anti-Symptomiasis. If you've read Kafka's *Metamorphosis* and thought, "Hey, I have that." And most importantly . . . if you find yourself automatically turning your head to cough in the middle of a handjob.

Of course, that's just my opinion, I could be wrong.

Where Is the Presidency Headed?

You know what the problem with the presidency is? We only pay the guy 250,000 bucks a year. You know, even NBA white guys make more than that.

Now, I don't want to get off on a rant here, but what is to become of our beloved presidency?

President Clinton's popularity is through the roof. All right, some of it's stuck on the ceiling. But it is through the roof. Partly because we like the job he is doing and partly because most Americans view those numbnuts in the Senate and the glass House of Representatives like they're the uptight frat guys from *Animal House*.

To me, the most interesting revelation to come out of the whole Lewinsky affair is that after a year in which the entire executive branch was supposedly hamstrung, the American people got along very nicely without it, thank you. Our Founding Fathers could never have predicted the absolute stability of our rudderless ship of state.

Oh and by the way, we have to stop viewing the presidency through the Rose Garden–colored glasses of the Constitution. Okay? Quit beating me over the head with this rolled-up 210-year-old "things to do" list.

Yeah, some of it's great. And some of it's just antiquated bullshit. Okay? Listen, if Thomas Jefferson were alive today and you drove him out to Washington National Airport in a BMW 700 series, put him on the Concorde, and gave him a laptop and a cell phone to fool around with for the *three and one half hour* flight to Europe, and then told him we were still running the country strictly according to the precepts he and his friends scribbled on a cocktail napkin once at a party in 1787, well, do you not think Jefferson would look at you in disbelief and say, "What the fuck are ye thinking?"

"Flip it over. See, it says right there, 'Feel free to change this every couple centuries or so, asshole.' "

Look, the office of the President has always functioned much like a frilly toothpick on a deli sandwich: It serves no nutritional purpose, but it looks good and holds things together.

For better or worse, a President embodies the sentiment and spirit of his time. And Clinton? Well, yeah, okay, compared to Clinton, eels are Velcro. But reprehensible as he is, we identify with him. Clinton's insatiable need to be loved, constantly undermined by his own self-destructive tendencies, is a larger-than-life parallel to our own inner turmoil. Ironically enough, it's now *we* who feel *his* pain.

In the near term, what will happen to the presidency depends on who we put into office. If we elect Al Gore, the President will be a dull, ineffectual figurehead from Tennessee. On the other hand, if we elect George Bush, Jr., the President will be a dull, ineffectual figurehead from Texas. See, that's why it's so vitally important that you vote. Because the letters after the "T" in the state they come from start to get different . . .

Hey, the presidency is not a Crisco orgy, but it's also not a platform for canonization, either. Okay? It's a job. And up until recently, it was one that respectable public servants might aspire to. And until we stop putting the chief executive's personal life under more scrutiny than Tyra Banks in a tae-bo class, the prospective pool of qualified applicants is going to be shallower than Jennifer Love Hewitt reciting some of her own poetry at the Virgin Megastore Café.

Look, folks, I hate to burst anybody's patriotic bubble, but there are no heroes anymore. The times we live in won't allow them. The very process of running for President is so debasing, it's guaranteed to squash whatever noble or idealistic impulses a candidate is naïve enough to entertain in the first place. I look at presidents the same way I do the guy who trims my hedges. All I ask is that he does his job, and doesn't rip me off, or stare too long at my wife. That's it.

I think if the next President is to learn anything from this whole episode, it's that he should be totally forthcoming with whatever dark secret he harbors, thereby completely defanging the rabid pack of partisan watchdogs nipping at his heels. You know, at this point I really believe that our entire nation actually *would* deify the first President who steps up to a podium, looks dead into a television camera, and says, "Folks, she blew me. As a matter of fact, she's blowing me right now. But enough about me. Let's talk about cutting yourrrrrrr—AHH! taxes."

Of course, that's just my opinion, I could be wrong.

Dennis Miller is the host of the five-time Emmy Award-winning "Dennis Miller Live" on HBO. He, his wife, and two children reside in California.

Printed in the United States
by Baker & Taylor Publisher Services